10° W.   0°   10° E.   60° N.

NORWAY

Bergen

SWEDEN

20° W.

NORTH SEA

DENMARK

BALTIC SEA

Kiel

GERMANY

SCOTLAND

SAPPHIRE

Glasgow

MARY

THE
NETHERLANDS

Amsterdam

The Hague

Rotterdam

50° N.

IRELAND

WALES

ENGLAND

London

Thames River

Calais

Cork

Southampton

Cowes

Le Havre

Paris

Isle of Wight

Cherbourg

Seine River

English Channel

ROYAL SOVEREIGN

FRANCE

VICTORIA AND ALBERT II

Monte Carlo

Marseilles

Barcelona

40° N.

Majorca

O C E A N

SPAIN

PORTUGAL

MEDITERRANEAN SEA

20° W.

10° W.

0°

The Seafarers THE LUXURY
YACHTS

TIME LIFE BOOKS ®

Other Publications:

LIBRARY OF HEALTH
CLASSICS OF THE OLD WEST
THE EPIC OF FLIGHT
THE GOOD COOK
THE ENCYCLOPEDIA OF COLLECTIBLES
THE GREAT CITIES
WORLD WAR II
HOME REPAIR AND IMPROVEMENT
THE WORLD'S WILD PLACES
THE TIME-LIFE LIBRARY OF BOATING
HUMAN BEHAVIOR
THE ART OF SEWING
THE OLD WEST
THE EMERGENCE OF MAN
THE AMERICAN WILDERNESS
THE TIME-LIFE ENCYCLOPEDIA OF GARDENING
LIFE LIBRARY OF PHOTOGRAPHY
THIS FABULOUS CENTURY
FOODS OF THE WORLD
TIME-LIFE LIBRARY OF AMERICA
TIME-LIFE LIBRARY OF ART
GREAT AGES OF MAN
LIFE SCIENCE LIBRARY
THE LIFE HISTORY OF THE UNITED STATES
TIME READING PROGRAM
LIFE NATURE LIBRARY
LIFE WORLD LIBRARY
FAMILY LIBRARY:
   HOW THINGS WORK IN YOUR HOME
   THE TIME-LIFE BOOK OF THE FAMILY CAR
   THE TIME-LIFE FAMILY LEGAL GUIDE
   THE TIME-LIFE BOOK OF FAMILY FINANCE

*This volume is one of a series
that celebrates the history of
maritime adventure, from the Greek
trireme to the modern ocean liner.*

The Cover: A far-roving behemoth
among modern-day luxury yachts was
William K. Vanderbilt Jr.'s 264-foot,
diesel-powered *Alva*, which he used during
the 1930s for pleasure cruises and
oceanographic expeditions around the
world. This painting was done by
William Belanske, employed by Vanderbilt
to portray marine specimens collected
during the yacht's oceanographic voyages.

The Title Page: A gilded figurehead
of England's Queen Charlotte, holding the
scepter of sovereignty, was carved in
1824, six years after her death, for a new
British royal yacht. It is a replica of the
figurehead on *Royal Charlotte*, the yacht
George III sent to bring her to England
from Germany for their marriage in 1761.

The Seafarers

THE LUXURY YACHTS

by John Rousmaniere
AND THE EDITORS OF TIME-LIFE BOOKS

TIME-LIFE BOOKS, ALEXANDRIA, VIRGINIA

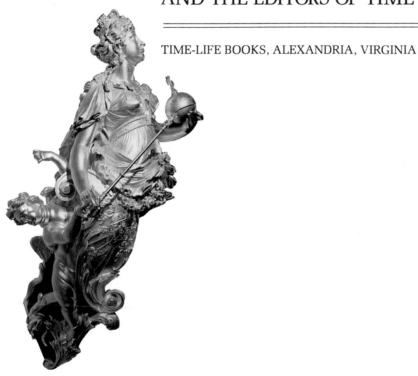

Time-Life Books Inc.
is a wholly owned subsidiary of
TIME INCORPORATED

FOUNDER: Henry R. Luce 1898-1967

Editor-in-Chief: Henry Anatole Grunwald
President: J. Richard Munro
Chairman of the Board: Ralph P. Davidson
Executive Vice President: Clifford J. Grum
Chairman, Executive Committee: James R. Shepley
Editorial Director: Ralph Graves
Group Vice President, Books: Joan D. Manley
Vice Chairman: Arthur Temple

TIME-LIFE BOOKS INC.

MANAGING EDITOR: Jerry Korn
Board of Editors: George Constable, George G. Daniels,
Thomas H. Flaherty Jr., Martin Mann, Philip W. Payne,
John Paul Porter, Gerry Schremp, Gerald Simons
Planning Director: Dale M. Brown
Art Director: Tom Suzuki
    Assistant: Arnold C. Holeywell
Director of Administration: David L. Harrison
Director of Operations: Gennaro C. Esposito
Director of Research: Carolyn L. Sackett
    Assistant: Phyllis K. Wise
Director of Photography: Robert G. Mason
    Assistant: Dolores A. Littles

CHAIRMAN: John D. McSweeney
President: Carl G. Jaeger
Executive Vice Presidents: John Steven Maxwell,
David J. Walsh
Vice Presidents: George Artandi, Stephen L. Bair,
Peter G. Barnes, Nicholas Benton, John L. Canova,
Beatrice T. Dobie, Carol Flaumenhaft, James L. Mercer,
Herbert Sorkin, Paul R. Stewart

The Seafarers

The Luxury Yachts was prepared under the supervision
of Time-Life Books by the following contributors:
Editors: Sheldon Cotler, A.B.C. Whipple
Picture Editor: Laurie Platt Winfrey
Assistant Designer: Leonard Vigliarolo
Researchers: Suzanne Odette Khuri, Susan Sivard,
Kaye Neil Noble, John E. Taktikos, Starr Badger Shippee,
Marian H. Mundy
Writers: R. H. Cravens, Harold C. Field,
Frederick King Poole, Cinda Siler, John Stickney
Art Assistant: Diana Raquel Vazquez
Editorial Manager: Felice Lerner
Editorial Assistants: Stacy Aronowitz,
Nicholas Goodman

Time-Life Books editorial staff for *The Luxury Yachts:*
Researcher: Patti H. Cass
Copy Coordinator: Anne T. Connell
Picture Coordinator: Jane A. Martin
Art Assistant: Robert K. Herndon

Editorial Operations
Production Director: Feliciano Madrid
    Assistants: Peter A. Inchauteguiz,
    Karen A. Meyerson
Copy Processing: Gordon E. Buck
Quality Control Director: Robert L. Young
    Assistant: James J. Cox
    Associates: Daniel J. McSweeney,
    Michael G. Wight
Art Coordinator: Anne B. Landry
Copy Room Director: Susan B. Galloway
    Assistants: Celia Beattie, Ricki Tarlow

Correspondents: Elisabeth Kraemer (Bonn);
Margot Hapgood, Dorothy Bacon (London); Susan Jonas,
Lucy T. Voulgaris (New York); Maria Vincenza Aloisi,
Josephine du Brusle (Paris); Ann Natanson (Rome).
Valuable assistance was provided by: Wibo van de Linde,
Bert Meijer, Jan Hovinga (Amsterdam); Mirka Gondicas
(Athens); Katrina Van Duyn (Copenhagen); Angi Lemmer
(Bonn); Judy Aspinall, Sylvia Pile, Jill Rose (London);
Cheryl Crooks (Los Angeles); Trini Bandres (Madrid);
Bruce Nelan, Felix Rosenthal (Moscow); Carolyn T.
Chubet, Miriam Hsia, Christina Lieberman, Gretchen
Wessels (New York); Dag Christensen (Oslo); Mimi
Murphy (Rome); Mary Johnson (Stockholm).

The Author:
John Rousmaniere has written four other
books on yachting, among them *A Glossa-
ry of Modern Sailing Terms,* and *Fastnet:
Force 10.* He is an avid yachtsman himself,
having twice sailed across the Atlantic. A
former associate editor of *Yachting* magazine, he also served as a consultant to the
Time-Life Library of Boating series.

The Consultants:
John Horace Parry, Gardiner Professor of
Oceanic History and Affairs at Harvard,
obtained his Ph.D. from Cambridge University. He is the author of many books on
seafaring, among them *The Discovery of
the Sea,* and *Trade and Dominion.*

Maldwin Drummond is both a maritime
historian and a veteran yachtsman who
has sailed European waters as well as the
Carribean, the Atlantic and the Pacific as
far south as Cape Horn. His books include
Salt Water Palaces, and he is the editor of
the *Royal Cruising Club Journal.*

James P. Shenton, Professor of History at
Columbia University, is a specialist in the
maritime and social history of the 19th
Century. Among his books are *These Unit-
ed States,* and *Free Enterprise Forever: the
Scientific American in the 19th Century.*

For information about any Time-Life book, please write:
Reader Information, Time-Life Books,
541 North Fairbanks Court, Chicago, Illinois 60611.

TIME-LIFE is a trademark of Time Incorporated U.S.A.

Library of Congress Cataloguing in Publication Data
Rousmaniere, John, 1944-
    The Luxury Yachts.
    (The Seafarers)
    Bibliography: p.
    Includes index.
    1. Yachts and yachting—History. I. Time-Life Books.
II. Series: Seafarers.
VM331.L89   623.8'223   81-9018   AACR2
ISBN 0-8094-2743-5
ISBN 0-8094-2744-3 (lib. bdg.)
ISBN 0-8094-2742-7 (retail ed.)

Contents

Showcases of splendor at sea

Almost by definition, a luxury yacht is a mansion afloat, designed to transport its owner in splendor and ease—and designed no less as proof of status and abundant means. Throughout history, monarchs and millionaires have gone to sea in sybaritic style, cosseted amid carved paneling and crystal chandeliers bearing no evident kinship to the nautical gear abovedecks. With the perfection of the marine steam engine in the latter part of the 19th Century, luxury yachts reached their zenith: Steam provided more stability and convenience than sail, and it supplied power adequate for vessels as large as any plutocrat could crave.

Four notable examples of belowdecks elegance are illustrated on these pages. *Invincible*, a steam yacht built in the United States in 1893, pampered her owner, diplomat Herbert G. Squiers, not only with a plush stateroom *(right)* but also with lavish sitting and dining saloons featuring plaster ceilings and electric lights. *Narcissus*, owned by British gentleman-landowner C. Oswald Liddell in the 1920s, boasted deep sofas, balustraded staircases and neo-Georgian fireplaces.

The Earl of Rosebury's *Zaida*, which he owned from 1901 until he chartered her to the Royal Navy in 1916, had teak bulkheads, wall-to-wall carpeting and the heavy upholstery of a town house. Another seaborne showplace was *North Star*, the pride of Cornelius Vanderbilt III, who named her after a steam yacht built for his great-grandfather in the mid-19th Century; Cornelius III bought this second *North Star* in 1902, and fitted her out with a degree of opulence deemed sufficient by his socialite wife, Grace, for entertainment of European royalty.

Leisure was not the full story of such vessels. During the golden age of luxury yachting, many owners commuted to and from work on their pleasure craft and even used them for traveling offices, maintaining radio communication with their shoreside headquarters. Indeed, it was a hallmark of such a yacht that, once aboard, the owner or guest could forget that he was at sea.

Invincible's stateroom displays the merest hint of its nautical nature—a rim for the dressing table to keep toiletries from sliding off.

Narcissus' saloon, endowed with a piano and an Oriental rug, was well lighted by outsized portholes and a skylight over the settee.

North Star's Louis XVI-style dining room provided a sumptuous setting for regatta cups won by her owner, Cornelius Vanderbilt III.

The writing room of the Earl of Rosebury's *Zaida* fostered a thoughtful mood with paneled walls, columns and a magnificent Chippendale desk.

Chapter 1

A royal instrument of statecraft

Henry VIII's majestic warship Henri-Grâce-à-Dieu (center) serves as his royal yacht during a ceremony in Dover in 1520.

I f dramatic impact can be counted among the hallmarks of luxury yachting, a high point of sorts occurred when Cleopatra's barge approached the Asia Minor port of Tarsus in 42 B.C. The historian Plutarch later wrote that, as the royal conveyance glided up the Cydnus River from the Mediterranean, the entire populace of the city rushed to the waterside. No vessel like this one had ever been seen before. The barge was propelled by rows of silver-sheathed paddles dipping in the river to a rhythm supplied by flutes, fifes and harps. From the vessel's short masts floated sails of purple linen, rippling in the breeze and providing more pageantry than propulsion. The sun flashed off the gilded stern. And shaded from the sun under a gold-embroidered canopy reclined the bewitching Queen of Egypt.

Cleopatra had been called to Tarsus—capital of the Roman province of Cilicia—by Mark Antony, ruler of the eastern portion of Rome's great Empire, to make sure that he had her support. But Cleopatra was no simple vassal to respond meekly to a Roman summons. She had taken her time in doing it, and now she was making sure that her arrival was a suitably imposing occasion.

Like an elaborate stage setting, the barge presented a tableau of ladies in waiting dressed as sea nymphs and goddesses of beauty. On either side of the canopy were two rows of boys dressed as cupids. Everyone was arranged so as to set off the central figure, lying languorously on her ornate couch. As the vessel moved across the river to Tarsus' main wharf, the crowds pouring out of the city could scent perfumed incense wafting from the deck.

Mark Antony was dispensing justice from a raised dais in the marketplace when Cleopatra's royal barge arrived. As he watched his audience disappear, he was amused rather than annoyed. He had encountered this clever and beguiling woman in Rome when she was Julius Caesar's mistress, and he was prepared for her theatricality. But even he, who controlled riches beyond measure and was accustomed to wielding power on a scale that any monarch might envy, could not help being impressed by her royal barge.

When Cleopatra invited him aboard for dinner, he readily accepted. He found the interior of the craft almost stupefyingly splendid, with scented air, purple-and-gold tapestried walls, and lights dancing off hundreds of burnished copper mirrors. On embroidered dining couches, the Roman and his vassal Queen ate from golden plates set with jewels and drank from golden goblets. By the time they came on deck again, the crew had hung the rigging with branches on which more lights shimmered in the soft Cilician night. Antony was captivated. Thereafter, he and Cleopatra would rarely be apart—although theirs would be an ill-fated union, ending in suicide after a failed bid for control of all of Rome's territories 11 years later.

It was no accident that a queen provided this epochal (if ultimately calamitous) demonstration of a yacht's power of dazzlement. For much of history, yachting was almost exclusively the privilege of kings, queens and nobles. Yachts served both as a comfortable mode of transportation and as a tool of statecraft—a symbol of power and wealth (in

Mesopotamian hieroglyphics dating back to 3000 B.C., the sign for "lord" was the bow of a ship).

The situation did not change until well into modern times. As late as the 18th Century, the British writer and naval officer, William Falconer, described a yacht in his *Universal Dictionary of the Marine* as a "vessel of state," adding that such a vessel was "usually employed to convey princes, ambassadors or other great personages from one kingdom to another." By his day, however, Falconer could make a distinction between a yacht and a royal yacht. The latter was "reserved for the sovereign"; it was "elegantly furnished and nobly ornamented with sculpture: and always commanded by captains in his majesty's navy. Besides these," Falconer pointed out, "there are many other yachts of a smaller kind, employed by the commissioners of the Excise, navy and customs; or used as pleasure-boats by private gentlemen."

As the Industrial Revolution generated new wealth, the trend toward a wider participation in this sport of kings would accelerate. The next century brought the development of yacht clubs, allowing owners to moor their pleasure craft in convivial splendor, and saw yachting spread to America, where prodigious fortunes were being accumulated. At the same time, the perfection of the steam engine opened the way to almost limitless comfort and grandeur. By the close of the 19th Century, yachtsmen were commissioning floating palaces hundreds of feet long and furnishing them in a style that made even Cleopatra's barge seem pedestrian by comparison. These beautiful behemoths would finally bring on their own demise by becoming so enormous (and so enormously expensive) that the worldwide Depression in the 1930s would render them obsolete—arrogant artifacts of a vanished age.

The beginnings of this seaborne parade of pomp and power can be traced—fittingly—to a ruler who was considered semidivine. The oldest known royal barge belonged to the Egyptian Pharaoh Cheops, who reigned in the middle of the Third Millennium B.C. Cheops' craft was rather plain; but she was commodious at 143 feet and had some rare comforts that evidently included an early version of air conditioning—dampened reed mats laid across the cabintop. The Pharaoh was so attached to his vessel that he had her buried alongside his tomb at Giza's Great Pyramid. Presumably the barge's last mission was to ferry Cheops to the afterworld.

From the Fourth Century B.C. on, Egypt was ruled by the Ptolemies, a Greek dynasty descended from a lieutenant of the world-conquering Alexander the Great. Ptolemy II built a whole fleet of royal yachts—all, according to the Greek historian Appian, "with gilded sterns and prows." His grandson Ptolemy IV had even bigger ideas. He ordered his shipwrights to construct a decked-over catamaran supporting a colonnaded palace that was 300 feet long and 45 feet wide and towered 60 feet above its water line. The riverborne palace, furnished in suitably opulent style, was towed up and down the Nile to make it more convenient for Ptolemy's subjects to pay their respects to their ruler.

The Romans displayed a similar flair for yachting. Their finest efforts were the work of the First Century Emperor Caligula, remembered chief-

One of the earliest royal yachts is preserved in this model, discovered in the tomb of Meket-Re, an Egyptian Pharaoh of the Second Millennium B.C. The wooden hull ends at bow and stern in a lotus motif, symbol of the kingdom of Egypt. Aft of the royal canopy, the helmsman handles two steering oars. On the foredeck, the crew raises the square-rigged mast; the support that held it in lowered position now lies on deck.

ly for a demented reign of terror. He commissioned several royal pleasure craft that were more than 200 feet long. Two of these yachts have been unearthed; both were painstakingly constructed with copper fastenings and lead sheathing to keep their hulls clean. Their amenities included reception chambers, exercise rooms, baths, a brothel and apparently even a grape arbor. The vessels' decks and companionways were paved with mosaics, lined with colored marble and decorated with bronze statues.

In 54 A.D., 13 years after Caligula's death, rule of Rome fell to Nero, an equally sensuous and homicidal Emperor: Among his many victims were his wife and his mother. Nero's royal barge was the scene of lavish banquets; the Emperor and his guests reclined on purple carpets while smaller gilt-and-ivory-decorated vessels towed the royal craft about a torch-lined lake and subjects provided a serenade from shore.

But neither Caligula nor Nero, imaginative as they were in providing for their pleasures, could match the extravagance of the second Emperor of the Sui Dynasty, Yang Ti, who reigned six centuries later in China.

Cleopatra's arrival at Tarsus to meet Mark Antony in 42 B.C. is depicted in this 15th Century painting by Neroccio de'Landi, who embellished the scene with medieval architecture and Renaissance costumes. While Cleopatra sits serenely on her throne and maidens line the deck, the populace rushes to see the spectacle— leaving Antony (left) nearly alone.

Emperor Yang Ti had a large fleet of royal junks, with a truly awesome yacht reserved for himself. One clearly exaggerated description claimed that she was 2,000 feet long, with four decks rising 40 feet above the water. Evidently she was painted crimson, because the Emperor whimsically called her *The Little Red.* Whatever her actual size—and it obviously was impressive—she resembled a palace inside the hull of a junk; in addition to a throne room for the Emperor's business of state and numerous suites, the yacht also had a 120-cabin harem. The Empress in her own enormous yacht accompanied the 50 or more dragon boats that regularly attended the Emperor's floating palace when he sailed about his kingdom.

Not content with the broad Yangtze, Emperor Yang Ti ordered the digging of a vast network of canals. More than five million workers were drafted to take part in the excavations. In some areas, every commoner between the ages of 15 and 50 was pressed into the labor force; for logistical support, every fifth family was required to contribute one family member to a supply corps that provided food for the laborers. Yang Ti

took full advantage of the canal system he had created: *The Little Red* and her accompanying armada of smaller junks were pulled along in grand processions by silk-clad workmen and young virgins straining on colored tow ropes. But the completion of the network cost two million lives, stirring such resentment that the people finally revolted and deposed the Emperor.

The institution of the royal yacht in Europe had spread north to Britain by the Seventh Century. On a heath near the River Deben in Suffolk, England, in an area now called Sutton Hoo, an Anglo-Saxon king was buried with an 89-foot funerary ship packed with gold coins and silver spoons and bowls for use in the afterlife. In Oseberg, Norway, in about 800, a Viking queen—thought to be Queen Asa—was entombed with a richly carved 70-foot vessel. A century later, a king of Norway found another use for a yacht; reasoning that it was the perfect gift for the monarch who had everything, he presented a purple-sailed longboat to King Athelstan of England in 925 A.D. This diplomatic example was followed a century later by King Earl Godwin of England, who gave a yacht to King Hardicanute of Denmark; she was bedecked in gilt, carried sails of royal purple and in calms or storms was rowed by 80 oarsmen wearing gold bracelets.

Oar power, which had been the main propulsion for all warships and many trading vessels since the beginnings of seafaring, was far from infallible. In the year 1120, the yacht of England's King Henry I, rowed by 50 oarsmen who had fortified themselves with wine, hit a rock and foundered. Crown Prince William, who was aboard, did not survive, and it was said that Henry was never seen to smile again. Still, oarsmen supplemented the purple sails that took Richard I's yacht *Trench le Mer* to Palestine during the Third Crusade seven decades later, and oarsmen helped Henry V's luxurious private warship, the *Trinity Royal*, speed across the English Channel to the battlefield of Agincourt some 200 years after that. By the end of the 16th Century, however, improvements in masts and rigging had rendered oared ships almost obsolete. When the Armada attempted an invasion of England in 1588, the few galleys in the Spanish fleet were almost helpless against the swift and maneuverable sailing ships of the foe.

After England's great victory, Queen Elizabeth commissioned a sailing yacht—called *Rat o' Wight* because of her diminutive size for a royal vessel. Elizabeth's successor, James I, also ordered a small sailing yacht, this one for his 10-year-old son Henry. She was only 28 feet long, but elaborate in her decor; her builder, Phineas Pett, noted that she was "garnished with painting and carving, both within board and without, very curiously according to his lordship's directions." In fact, she was a miniature version of the ship of the line *Ark Royal*, which had fought gallantly against the Armada. The young Prince in 1604 named his elaborate plaything *Disdain*, after another veteran of the Armada, and liked her so much that his father some years later asked Pett to build the lad a larger yacht; Henry died of typhoid fever before she was finished.

Henry's younger brother, who succeeded to the throne as Charles I, was less interested in the pleasures of the sea. But Charles's son and namesake would usher in a new era in yachting. For him, sailing in

Emperor Yang Ti, said to have owned 30,000 royal yachts in the Seventh Century A.D., organized grand flotillas on China's canals. An 18th Century Chinese artist here re-creates one of the processions, with a dragon-prowed royal yacht being pulled alongshore, escorted by flag-carrying royal troops, as a yacht in the background waits its turn.

luxurious vessels was not just a perquisite of his exalted position; it was also a passionate avocation. Yachting truly became a royal sport.

Charles Stuart was a man of many interests, one of the greatest of which was the sea. That came about partly by force of circumstance. When he was 16 years old, his father's reign was threatened by the followers of Oliver Cromwell. Charles at first fought alongside his father; but as defeat became more certain and rumors of a possible kidnapping attempt spread, he was ordered to flee to the Scilly Isles, off Cornwall, where he whiled away a month and a half sailing a small boat. When rebel privateers nosed into the area, Charles went southeast, taking the helm of the frigate *Proud Black Eagle* as she carried him to the island of Jersey, off the coast of France. There he settled into a watery refuge, Elizabeth Castle, which was cut off by every high tide. Soon he commissioned his first yacht, borrowing money from the island's Governor in order to pay for her. As he sailed about the island, he became an addicted yachtsman.

By now, the once-spoiled young Prince had matured into a hardened 18-year-old, six feet two inches tall, tested in battle and conscious of the responsibility that would devolve on him if his father's cause were lost. It was lost in 1649; Charles I was dethroned and beheaded. And his son moved to avenge him.

Sailing to Leith, Scotland, the new King gathered a Scottish army and marched south. In three weeks he had reached Worcester, within 100 miles of London. But by then his ragtag army of 16,000 was exhausted, and Cromwell's 30,000 men defeated them in a bloody battle. Again Charles was a fugitive—and again he headed for the sea. Traveling incognito, sleeping in barns—and one night in the branches of a tree—he reached the village of Brighthelmstone (now Brighton) on England's south coast. There he managed to charter the 31-foot coal brig *Surprise*, which took him and a handful of followers across the English Channel to France. For the next nine years he lived on the Continent.

During that time, Cromwell's harshness and the country's declining economy made Englishmen long for the return of the monarchy. As reports of unrest and possible uprising reached Charles, he moved closer to the coast so that he would be ready for a triumphant return to his homeland. He was at Hoogstraeten, in the Spanish Netherlands, playing tennis, when he received news of Cromwell's unexpected death in 1658. But 19 more months passed before the Commonwealth finally collapsed and Parliament prepared to call the exiled King home again. Charles was ready, waiting in Breda, Holland. And when he learned that a deputation from Parliament was on its way to The Hague, he decided to go there—by yacht.

During his visit to the Netherlands, Charles grew fond of the Dutch, not least because of their maritime tradition. Holland—more accurately, the Seven United Provinces of the Northern Netherlands—was the first great mercantilist European nation to earn its wealth from the sea, and by the mid-17th Century it was the trading center of Europe, with more merchant ships than all the other European nations combined. So affluent had the Dutch become that many of them could afford craft intended purely for pleasure. They called them *jaght schips*.

A glittering galley for the Sun King

The ancient galley of the Mediterranean was perpetuated into the 16th and 17th Centuries by the kings of France, who used elaborate versions of the vessel—propelled by both oar and sail—for their yachts. The largest were powered by more than 200 men on a side; one such yacht was 170 feet long and 21 feet across.

Each of the royal yachts was called *La Réale*, and some served as flagship of the Navy as well as the King's pleasure craft. But they were more ornamental than efficient. Although the galleys' low freeboard suited conditions in the Mediterranean well enough, the decks were awash most of the time in the open Atlantic—and when the yachts' larger sails made them heel, the leeward oarsmen were waist-deep in rushing water. These outmoded vessels finally gave way to oarless sailing ships—but not until Louis XIV crowned their long history with the stunning expression of regal magnificence seen here.

Adornments worthy of the creator of Versailles bespangle Louis XIV's yacht, built near the end of the 17th Century (and shown in these drawings with her oars shipped and her sails furled). At sea, the King reposed under the broad awning over the poop deck.

Despite a deep keel, Louis XIV's Réale was top-heavy, a condition exacerbated by platforms, extending on each side of her stern, that provided for regal debarking but were impractical in a heavy sea.

Vue de la Poupe de la Galere-Réale.

FRANCE'S LOUIS XIV

The Dutch word *jaght* originally meant "hunt": A *jaght vogel* was a hunting bird similar to the quick-striking falcon. The word's connotation of speed somehow seemed to fit the swift little pleasure craft in which the wealthy burghers of Holland skimmed across the Zuider Zee and up and down the canals of their sea-girt land.

As Dutch prosperity increased, so did the size of the *jaght schips*: Some measured as much as 115 feet at the water line. They were beamy, commodious, shallow-draft vessels, generally sloop-rigged and fitted with leeboards to keep them from sideslipping. Paying homage to the prestigious Dutch Navy by imitation, the yachts carried cannon, and their owners liked to assemble in grand processions and even engage in mock naval battles.

Charles had become fascinated by the handsome, maneuverable *jaght schips*. Since a large portion of his 45-mile trip to The Hague would be by canal and river, the Dutch offered him the loan of a yacht. On the voyage his vessel was accompanied by a gala fleet of a dozen other yachts, all of them outfitted with elegant accommodations, often including elaborate kitchens capable of providing a banquet en route. A Dutchman who accompanied the royal party wrote:

"Each yacht had her own steward, cooks, and officers, who were in charge of the pantry, kitchen, and wines, and those yachts that had not suitable kitchens on board were accompanied by other vessels, wherein stoves for the kitchen had been provided, also ovens for baking, and there had been made provisions of so great a quantity of all kinds of food, game, comfitures, and wines, and all the tables were so fully served, that the stewards of the English lords, though accustomed to abundance, were astonished thereat, and confessed that they could not conceive by what means 20 or 25 great dishes for each table could be prepared on board the yachts and with the motion of the water."

Charles no doubt enjoyed the feast on his yacht, but his sister Mary, who accompanied him, did not. The procession was scarcely under way when a freshening breeze kicked up enough of a chop, even in the relatively protected bay of the Dovdtse Kil, to make her seasick. The wind increased, the shallow-draft vessel rolled, and Mary grew worse, spending several miserable hours belowdecks. Charles, meanwhile, promenaded the deck in high spirits, studying the yacht and admiring her. Before the voyage was over, his heart was set on possessing a pleasure craft of this very type, and he asked if he could purchase such a vessel. The Dutch Board of Admiralty gladly presented him with one.

She was 52 feet long, with a 19-foot beam. Her draft was three feet, extended to 10 feet when her leeboards were down. Her interior was lavishly furnished; a contemporary noted that the yacht's donors "had the interior of the cabins decorated and gilded, while some of the best artists have been engaged in making beautiful paintings and sculptures with which to embellish it within and without."

Charles returned home in May of 1660, traveling in a more appropriate vessel, the English 80-gun man-of-war *Naseby*, which was renamed *Royal Charles* for the occasion. His yacht meanwhile was put through sailing trials, arriving at her Whitehall wharf on the Thames in August of the same year. Charles named her *Mary*, after his sister, and was so

England's first royal yachtsman, Charles II, owned a large fleet of pleasure craft during his reign (1660-1685). Eager to improve the performance of his yachts, Charles was criticized by one observer for knowing about shipbuilding "rather more than became a prince."

pleased with her that he immediately ordered another, this one to be built locally. Shipwright Peter Pett, son of Phineas, went aboard the Dutch yacht to study her lines; he was accompanied by the naval clerk and diarist Samuel Pepys, who wrote, "Mr. Pett is to make one to outdo this for the honour of his country, which I fear he will scarce better." Pett managed to satisfy his sovereign, who named the new yacht *Catherine*, after his bride-to-be. His brother James, Duke of York, thereupon commissioned a similar vessel. By the spring of 1661 the King and the Duke were happily sailing their yachts together on the Thames.

Charles II was a patron of poets and painters, and a supporter of England's first scientific establishment, the Royal Society. At the same time, he indulged his taste for luxury and pleasure without stint, earning the appellation of "the Merry Monarch." He was an avid collector of clocks and other mechanical devices, of horses and dogs, of mansions and mistresses—and, particularly, of yachts: In the quarter century of his reign he had at least 26 of them.

All were visions of opulence, with elaborately gilded bulwarks and soaring poop decks. Some had ornate figureheads, usually in the form of a bird's head. Nearly all mounted guns, mostly for decoration and for firing salutes; many of the gunports were encircled by wreaths of gilded wood. Besides the customary signal flags, the royal yachts carried a full inventory of large silk ceremonial flags; they accounted for more than 10 per cent of the yachts' cost. And belowdecks, Charles's yachts were almost as sumptuous as his palaces. Bulkheads were paneled in mahogany; crimson damask hung at the portholes and around the beds. Such appointments as Holland quilts and pewter chamber pots added to the ambiance—and to the price. The cost of a warship at that time was about £15 per ton, a merchant vessel £8 per ton; one of Charles's yachts cost about £33 per ton.

Adding to the expense of the royal hobby were the salaries of the 10 to 40 naval officers and men who served aboard each yacht. Since the King's considerable income rarely was sufficient for his extravagances, Charles tried to talk the Royal Navy into maintaining his fleet of yachts. In this effort, however, he met with only middling success.

Navy obstinacy was not the only curb on this most sporting of kings. By the middle of the 1660s, the pressures of mercantile rivalry led to intermittent war with the Dutch—a development that must have pained the Dutch Board of Admiralty officials who had curried Charles's favor a few years earlier. And the devastating combination of an outbreak of plague and the great London fire of 1666 made yachting seem inconsequential even to Charles II. But by the 1670s, England had recovered sufficiently for him to return to his favorite avocation. Thirteen of the royal yachts were commissioned in this decade (two of them were lent to the Royal Navy for the first thorough survey of the waters around Britain). And Charles continued to cruise the Thames almost until his death in 1685, a passionate lover of the sea to the end.

The next great royal yachtsman bore a number of similarities to Charles, although he was no relation. Russia's Czar Peter the Great was not only outsized in stature—six feet seven inches tall—but a man of extraordinary mental and physical vigor. And the sea would always be a prime arena for his boundless energies.

To Peter's contemporaries, it must have seemed unlikely in the extreme that any Russian ruler would ever turn to yachting. In the late 17th Century, his country contained more territory than any in the world. Yet Russia was by far the most backward of Europe's nations. She was remote, if not impenetrable, and lacked any real access to the sea.

In the south, Russia was blocked from the Black Sea by savage Tartar vassals of the Ottoman Empire, and the Caspian Sea was controlled by Persia. In the west the Swedes had turned the Baltic into their own lake. In the Far East, the Chinese had taken control of the Amur River mouth, Russia's outlet to the Seas of Okhost and Japan. The only Russian seaport was at Archangel, on the White Sea, 130 miles below the Arctic Circle and blocked by ice for more than half the year.

Not only was there no Russian navy, there was very little interest in one. The Russians themselves built no seagoing ships of any kind and were not sailors. Not one Russian czar had ever stood on the deck of a craft sailing on salt water. A czar was expected, except when leading

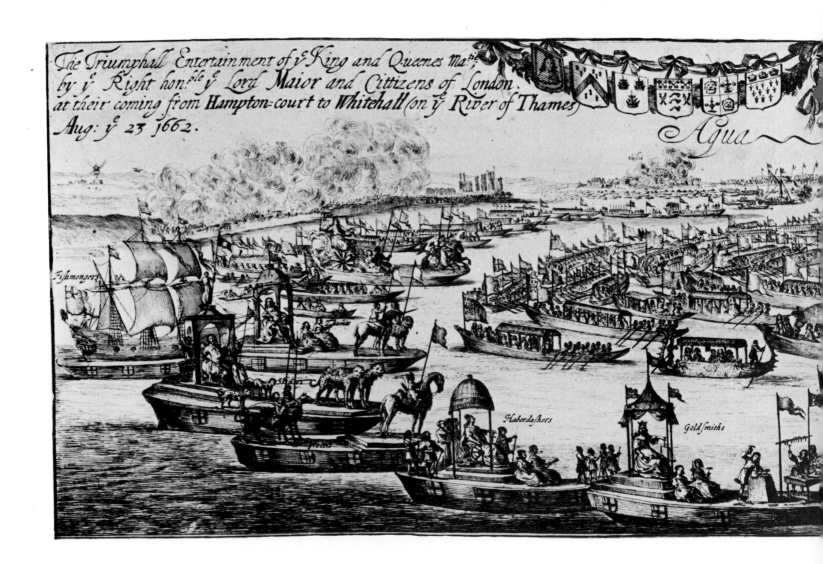

troops into battle, to preside over his vast empire from the Kremlin, where he sat in Oriental splendor, dazzling an endless stream of visitors with his gigantic jeweled crown and scepter.

Although he was as autocratic as his predecessors, Peter hated the trappings and ceremony of his role. He avoided the Kremlin whenever he could. He dressed casually and preferred an informal life among his cronies, laughing, joking and drinking, often to excess. As his moods shifted, he could turn violent and cruel, assaulting his friends, casually ordering torture and execution for his enemies. Uneducated in the academic sense, he had an intense fascination with anything practical and mechanical. More than anything else, he loved working with his hands. By his early teens Peter had become a skilled carpenter, stonemason and blacksmith; throughout his life he would escape from his court to indulge in such trades and try countless others—everything from watchmaking to navigation.

As a youth, Peter lived under a regency; not until he was 17 did he force his relatives aside and seize complete power. A year before that, he had found a new focus for his life. Peter had struck up a friendship with a

A contemporary etching records the waterborne procession as Charles II presents his new Queen, Catherine, to London in 1662. The King and Queen, under a golden canopy in the royal barge (upper center), are escorted by gilded floats while spectators watch from elaborate barges (foreground).

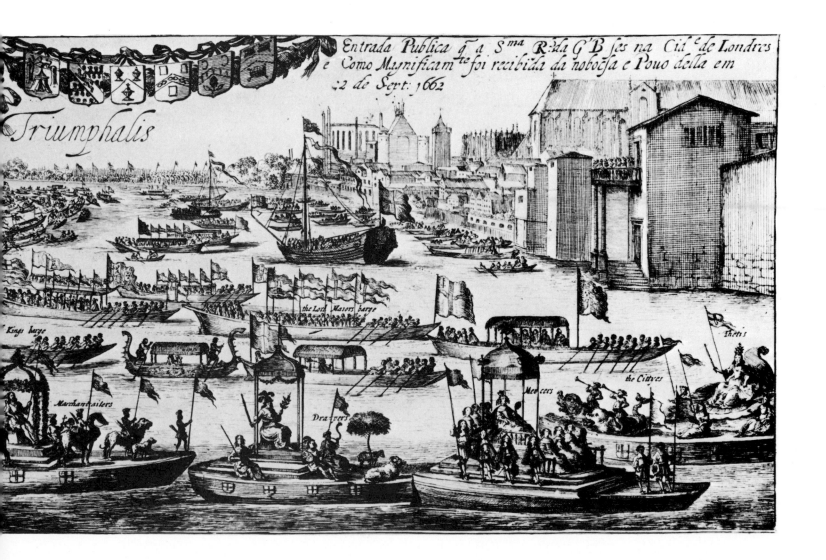

Dutch merchant named Franz Timmerman, with whom the young Czar liked to explore the royal estates outside Moscow. Poking about in a storehouse one day, they found the warped hull of a 20-foot-long, six-foot-wide sailing craft, said to have been sent by Queen Elizabeth of England as a gift to Ivan the Terrible, a despot of the previous century.

At this time Peter had seen no body of water bigger than a village pond, and the only boats in his experience were the clumsy-looking, squared-off, flat-bottomed craft that were rowed or pulled with ropes from the banks along Russia's rivers. But this English craft, with a pointed bow, a deep, rounded hull and a heavy keel, was clearly meant for something more exciting. Timmerman explained to the enthralled young Czar how, with the proper sails and rigging, she could actually sail against currents and tack against the wind.

With the help of a Dutch worker who had shipbuilding skills, Peter and his mentor replaced the vessel's rotted timbers, calked the hull, erected a new mast and rigged it with sails. Then they took the boat on rollers to the nearby Yauza River. Soon Peter was spending his days sailing. But the river was too tame for him. He longed for open water.

The largest body of water near the capital was Lake Pleschev, nine miles across. But it lay 85 miles to the northeast—too far to transport the English boat. So Peter decided to create his own shipyard. Soon he was wielding axes, hammers and chisels from dawn to dusk with other workers, most of them imported Dutchmen familiar with shipbuilding. The Czar's plans were characteristically ambitious: He laid keels for two small frigates and three yachts. So large a fleet on Lake Pleschev had no practical use, but the Czar was interested in learning how to construct various types of vessels. He lived in workers' huts, labored as hard as a serf and dressed in old Western clothes and battered boots. His choice of attire in fact heralded one of his later moves to Westernize Russia: In time he would ban the traditional long Russian robes as impractical, having discovered himself that they hindered his movements when he worked and sailed.

By the time he was 20, Peter's lake flotilla consisted of a dozen craft. But this was still the stuff of a child's fantasies. The next year, 1693, he decided to try a real sea.

That summer he and his Dutch friends, plus some members of the court, traveled a thousand miles north to the White Sea. At Archangel— never before visited by a czar—Peter mingled with English and Dutch seamen. He worked on the wharves and at forges and lathes. Before the summer was over he had his first seagoing yacht, which he called St. Peter. She became the first Russian naval ship, since he used her to escort Dutch and English merchantmen through the White Sea to the Arctic Ocean. He also used her simply for voyages of pleasure.

During a cruise aboard this yacht in the company of an archbishop and some courtiers, the Czar encountered a violent gale. The yacht's sails were torn off her mast, and huge waves swept over her bow and along her deck. As she wallowed and pitched, Peter's companions and even the veteran crewmen turned to prayer. The archbishop gave the final blessing to everyone, including Peter. But the Czar, evidently managing to rig a storm sail, took the helm, gauging each onrushing wave and guiding his yacht to meet it head on. For nearly 24 hours he fought the storm. Finally, with the help of the pilot, he found a port of refuge, the harbor of Unskaya Gulf. In a wild dash he took *St. Peter,* as the wind sent her flying, through a channel between surf-smothered rock outcroppings and brought his yacht to a safe anchorage.

The narrow escape only whetted Peter's love of sailing. He had already commissioned—and helped build—a new yacht, which he named *St. Paul.* Meanwhile he sent an order to Holland for a 44-gun frigate to be built for him and sent to Archangel. When he came back to the White Sea the next spring, he brought along 300 attendants and took possession of *St. Paul* and the frigate. Russia now had a fledgling naval fleet.

If he were to have an effective navy, however, Peter needed year-round access to the sea. He launched a campaign against the Tartars blocking him from the Black Sea, but was only temporarily successful. He then set his sights on the Baltic—and to assure success he dispatched the sons of the Russian nobility to Holland, England and Venice for naval training.

In 1697 the Czar himself visited the West. His aides regarded the trip as a diplomatic and educational venture. Peter turned it into a yachtsman's holiday. He first went to Holland, where he insisted on working as a carpenter in a shipyard in Zaandam, a shipbuilding center. He also bought a sailboat, rerigging it himself with a new mast and bowsprit. Although he tried to conceal his identity by using the name of Peter

Mary, the gift of the Dutch to the newly crowned Charles II of England, was decorated with a unicorn figurehead and gilded carvings at her high stern. Built according to Dutch style, the yacht had leeboards (center) to keep her from sideslipping when sailing into the wind.

Mikhailov, rumors of his presence spread, and his great height gave him away. In consequence, whenever he went sailing on the Ij River, other boats gathered around him.

To escape the curious Zaandamers he traveled to the capital, Amsterdam. There he was recognized by the city's officials, who entertained him in state. Peter's hosts, however, found their Russian visitor unschooled in diplomatic niceties: At banquets he drank too much and ate with his hands. So no one objected when Peter retreated to a Dutch East India Company shipyard. He settled into simple lodgings nearby and reported to the shipyard every morning at dawn with the rest of the ships' carpenters, his tools slung over his shoulders. His Dutch hosts saw to it that the keel of a new frigate was laid down for him, and Peter worked happily on her hull and rigging. Legend has it that a foreign ambassador, visiting Amsterdam to pay his respects to the Czar of Russia, was directed first to the shipyard, then up into the frigate's rigging. In the crosstrees, Peter—a tar bucket hanging from his neck—accepted the ambassador's credentials with black, sticky hands.

On September 1, 1697, Holland's chief Navy officer, Admiral Gilles Schey, produced a spectacle that Peter never forgot: one of Holland's elaborate mock naval battles. Every Dutchman with a yacht was invited to take part, and several hundred turned out. The event took place on a sunny Sunday and in a perfect breeze. Admiral Schey divided the yachts into two squadrons. The Navy provided cannon, gunpowder (but presumably no cannonballs) and soldiers with muskets for those yachts large enough to accommodate them. While the opposing lines of battle faced each other, the flagship of the East India Company, with Peter aboard, reviewed them and received their salutes. Then the admiral hoisted a red flag; a gun sounded, and the two squadrons went into action. Wrote an observer: "The fleet began very well-directed maneuvers; and, after having kept their course for some time, they passed alongside one another in perfect line, firing their cannon with great energy, the charges being enlarged a great deal, to give more show and importance to the battle."

Other sources indicate that the mock battle got slightly out of hand and had to be called off when some of the yachts, manned by overenthusiastic crews, collided with one another. Meanwhile, the guest of honor had worked himself up to "a state of rapture difficult to describe," according to another spectator, and ordered the captain of his yacht to sail into the middle of the fray. The Czar was so impressed by the mock battle that he later offered Admiral Schey a title and a large amount of money if he would move to Russia and supervise the commissioning of the navy Peter was planning. Schey politely declined. But Peter's hosts made up for the disappointment by giving the Czar the frigate on which he had been working in the Amsterdam shipyard.

In Holland, Peter met an important Westerner who would further encourage his yen for yachting. William of Orange, King of England, was also still Stadholder—Governor—of his native United Netherlands. He had held this latter title when some members of England's Parliament invited him to cross the Channel and assume the British crown. William's links to Britain were his mother, Mary, daughter of Charles I, and

An elegant figure clad in his royal armor (right), Russia's Czar Peter the Great preferred to wear workingmen's clothes and engage in his favorite hobby, shipbuilding. On a state visit to Holland during the 1690s, the Czar grew a beard, donned a laborer's cap (above) and worked in an Amsterdam shipyard.

his wife, also named Mary, niece of Charles II. On Charles's death in 1685, his brother James had succeeded to the throne; but James had fallen into disfavor with Parliament's dominant Protestants, who felt threatened by the King's active Catholicism. William of Orange led his troops against the King—whose own troops deserted him. James fled to France; Parliament ruled his flight an abdication, and in 1689 William and Mary assumed the throne in what English historians labeled the Glorious Revolution.

William frequently revisited his homeland, and he happened to be in Holland during the visit of Peter the Great. The rough-hewn young Russian giant and the short, stooped, 47-year-old statesman made a curiously contrasting pair. William knew the way straight to Peter's heart: He promised him a new yacht.

The Czar was ready by now for a visit to England. He felt he had learned all he could in Holland. By William's arrangement, the man-of-war H.M.S. *Yorke*, with an admiral in command, put into Amsterdam in January of 1689 to pick Peter up. The ship proceeded into the English Channel—and into a wild winter storm. While his aides lay in their bunks below, hanging on and retching as the *Yorke* rolled and pounded through the heavy seas, the Czar stayed on deck. His heavy Dutch seaman's clothes were drenched with icy spray, but Peter was thrilled by the gale's power. He even climbed the slippery rigging, inviting the English admiral to join him. The admiral begged off, pleading that he had become too fat for that sort of thing.

Twenty-four hours later, a still-excited Czar finally sighted the Suffolk shoreline and received a gratifying salute from the guns of the coastal fort. At the mouth of the Thames, Peter boarded the King's yacht *William and Mary* and, escorted by two more royal yachts, sailed upriver to London Bridge. A state barge took him on the last leg of his procession, to land on a quay at the Strand and be greeted by the court chamberlain.

Quickly bored with ceremony, Peter tried to resume an incognito existence, selecting as his lodgings a small house overlooking the Thames. His desire for anonymity was not helped by the King's insistence on visiting him. (William found the Czar in shirt sleeves, sharing his bedroom with four of his traveling companions.) Finally, Peter retreated down the Thames to the shipbuilding town of Deptford. There he resided at elegant Sayes Court, the country house of the essayist and diarist John Evelyn. Its owner had spent 45 years landscaping the grounds and furnishing the house to his very refined tastes—an effort undone in three months by Peter and his rowdy companions. The garden fences and more than 50 chairs were used as fuel in the stoves and fireplaces. Carpets were ruined and floors so stained with grease that they had to be replaced. Brass door locks were pried open (no doubt to see how they worked). Some 300 windowpanes were broken. Feather beds, pillows, sheets and canopies were ripped apart, evidently in colossal pillow fights. All of the paint work was ruined. The Russians also discovered a new sport: racing wheelbarrows. Each wheelbarrow carried one of the roisterers, and the racecourse led through the flower beds and the formal holly hedges. The gardens were all but destroyed.

But if Peter's evenings were given over to carousing, his days were

A state yacht fires a salute to the man-of-war Golden Lion,
while other yachts whisk about Amsterdam harbor in a scene
painted by William van de Velde the Younger in 1686.

dutifully spent in manual labor in one of Deptford's shipyards while he awaited delivery of his yacht. Finally, on March 2, nearly two months after his arrival, she was ready. William christened her *Royal Transport*; her specifications have been lost, but she carried 20 brass cannon and almost certainly was faster than any of the Czar's Russian-built yachts.

Not to be outdone by Peter's hosts in Holland, William staged a mock naval battle in the waters of the Solent, between the Isle of Wight and the south coast of England. Although he probably would have preferred to take part aboard *Royal Transport*, Peter was persuaded to view the spectacle from the man-of-war *Humber*. He nonetheless enjoyed himself thoroughly. As the broadsides of Royal Navy vessels thundered across the Solent, Peter ecstatically made notes of the signal flags, the maneuvers and the gun drills.

By May it was time to return home. The King reimbursed John Evelyn for the destruction of his country house with the then-large sum of £350. It is said that Peter reimbursed William for both that payment and the yacht by casually reaching into his pocket and taking out a huge uncut diamond, which he presented to the King as a parting gift.

Peter at last set out across the Channel for Amsterdam, escorted by a Royal Navy squadron. This time the Channel was even stormier; again Peter's companions went moaning to their bunks while the Czar kept the helm, enjoying each spray-flying plunge into the mountainous seas.

It was his last sail in the yacht. From Holland, Peter went overland to Moscow, while *Royal Transport,* laden with his gifts and purchases—including the latest navigational equipment, texts on seamanship, globes, charts, maps—was brought around the tip of Europe into the Arctic and down to Archangel. But her draft was too deep to pass through some of Russia's smaller rivers. She sat at her wharf in Archangel for 15 years. Peter had grandiose plans to link the larger rivers with deep canals so that vessels with as much draft as *Royal Transport* could navigate inland. But for the time being, his energies were taken up by military and naval matters. Not until 1715 did he order *Royal Transport* brought westward around the North Cape to meet him in the Baltic Sea. Off Marstrand, on the west coast of Sweden, she ran into a storm that sent her to the bottom.

The Czar had meanwhile turned his attention to the Baltic. In 1703, on land he had conquered at the mouth of the Neva River, he began laying out St. Petersburg, which would be Russia's capital for more than two centuries. After his forces swept Swedish garrisons from the Russian shores of the Baltic, he established shipyards to build a naval fleet—again appearing in person from time to time to labor as a skilled workman. Within two decades Russia dominated the Baltic with 34 ships of the line, 15 frigates and 800 oared galleys—ideal for pillaging Swedish settlements along the coasts. The best ships, one observer claimed, equaled those of England and "were more handsomely furnished."

Despite this extraordinary achievement, the Navy was largely staffed by foreigners. Although there were now some Russian-born admirals, members of the nobility often went to great lengths to avoid naval service, faking illness or even going into exile. Peter was one of the few Russians on any social level in his inward-looking country who did not

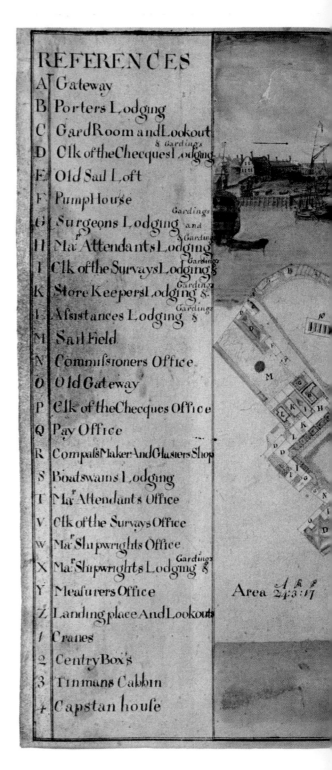

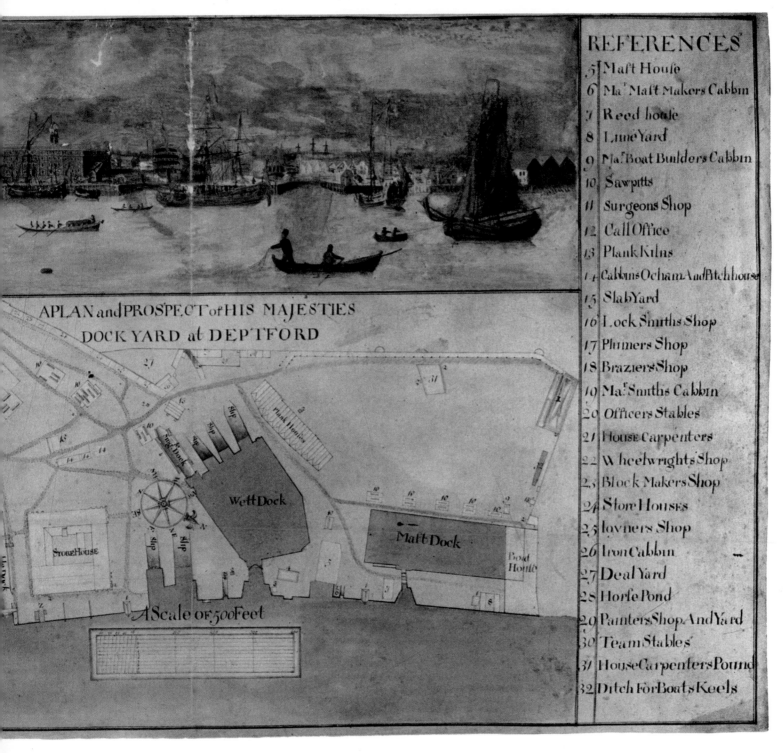

APLAN and PROSPECT of HIS MAJESTIES
DOCK YARD at DEPTFORD

Wett Dock

Maft Dock

StoreHouse

Boat Houfe

A Scale of 500 Feet

REFERENCES

5	Maft Houfe
6	Ma.r Maft Makers Cabbin
7	Reed houfe
8	Lime Yard
9	Ma.r Boat Builders Cabbin
10	Sawpitts
11	Surgeons Shop
12	Call Office
13	Plank Kilns
14	Cabbins Ocham And Pitch houfe
15	Slab Yard
16	Lock Smiths Shop
17	Plimers Shop
18	Braziers Shop
19	Ma.r Smiths Cabbin
20	Officers Stables
21	House Carpenters
22	Wheelwrights Shop
23	Block Makers Shop
24	Store Houses
25	Joyners Shop
26	Iron Cabbin
27	Deal Yard
28	Horse Pond
29	Painters Shop And Yard
30	Team Stables
31	House Carpenters Pound
32	Ditch For Boats Keels

The Royal Dockyards at Deptford,
on the south bank of the Thames near
London, are shown in this combination
painting and detailed diagram done in
the 18th Century. Established in
1513, the Yard built royal yachts as well
as Navy ships for 300 years. Most of
the vessels were built and launched in the
finger-like basins at the diagram's center.

actually hate the sea. He had accomplished Russia's rise to major status as a naval power almost singlehandedly.

But for Peter, sailing was never a duty. Toward the end of his life, an English visitor wrote that the Czar "has often declared to his lords, when he had been a little merry, that he thinks it a much happier life to be an admiral in England than a tsar in Russia." By now Peter had many yachts, which he sailed on the Neva River and in the Gulf of Finland; he owned homes on the waterfront where he could moor them. In 1723 the Prussian Ambassador complained that Peter "is so occupied with his villas and sailing on the gulf that none has the heart to interrupt him."

A year earlier Peter had ordered that his first yacht, the English sailboat he had discovered when he was a teenager, be hauled overland to St. Petersburg. For much of the journey from Moscow the sailboat was dragged over log roads. "Be careful not to destroy it," Peter cautioned. "For this reason go only in daytime. Stop at night. When the road is bad, be especially careful."

In August 1723, two years before Peter's death, the 20-foot boat that had helped change the destinies of the Czar and his people sailed in the Gulf of Finland flying the imperial standard and with Peter himself at the tiller and four admirals manning oars. It was saluted with salvos from the great Russian ships of the line. And that summer it was brought

Regal accommodations are revealed in this cross section of a 17th Century Stuart royal yacht, probably belonging to Charles II. The Great Cabin amidships had paintings on the wall and an overhead skylight. The royal cabins on the upper deck aft of the central cabin included the King's stateroom (left) and the Queen's more lavish quarters, with elaborate draperies and a huge four-poster bed.

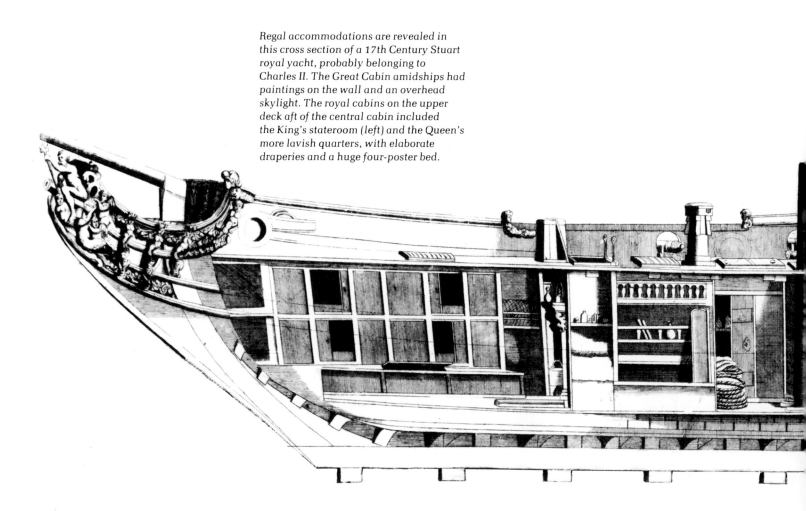

ashore and given a permanent berth of honor inside St. Petersburg's Fortress of Peter and Paul. This little craft, said Peter, was nothing less than "the Grandfather of the Russian Navy."

Peter the Great and Charles Stuart were unusual in their attachment to the sea and their passion for the sporting side of yachting. Among monarchs, yachting remained popular—especially in England—but generally took a ceremonial and sedate form. For instance, after George III assumed the throne of England in 1760, he made frequent use of yachts (he ultimately had five in all) for naval reviews, pageants and parades. These were troubled times, with England embroiled in wars against France and her own American colonies, and the King believed in making the royal presence felt so as to bolster the morale of the Navy.

In February 1801, George III had a severe attack of what has since been diagnosed either as a manic-depressive psychosis or as porphyria, a rare hereditary metabolic disorder affecting the brain. The King babbled excitedly, starting a new sentence before he was able to finish the last, often talking to himself. He cried out in the night, was unable to remain still and unable to sleep. His ravings were accompanied by fever, intestinal disorders and failing vision. Still, between bouts of insanity, his life went on as usual, and he continued to show himself to his subjects

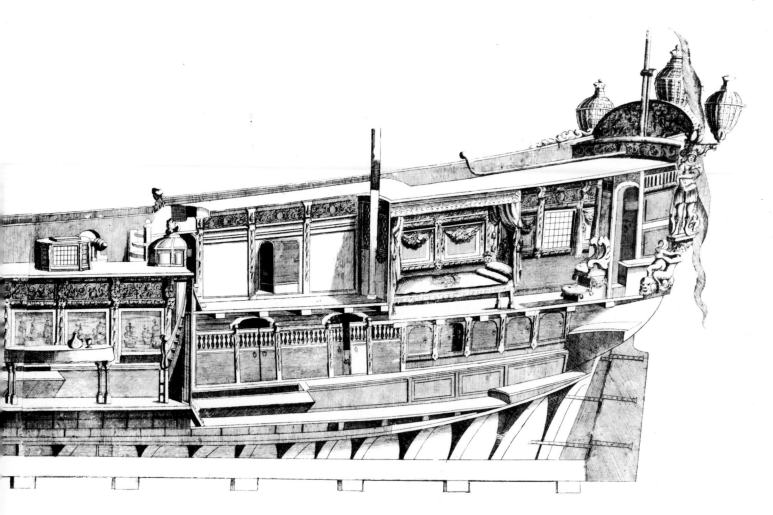

aboard his yachts and to take occasional pleasure trips to the seaside resort of Weymouth, on England's south coast.

One of his lucid acts was to order the grandest new yacht of his fleet. *Royal Sovereign*, as she was christened in 1804, was a 278-tonner. She was ship-rigged, and her hull was a veritable cathedral of decorative symbolism. On her topsides were gilded medallions representing the four cardinal virtues as female figures; on her transom was a representation of Neptune in his chariot, with dolphins swimming around him. Carvings of the four corners of the world abounded. *Royal Sovereign's* figurehead was a bust of Queen Charlotte, and sweeping aft from the bow were yellow and blue stripes.

Belowdecks she was even more luxuriant. Wrote a reporter for *The Times:* "The after-cabin is elegantly inlaid with damask panels ornamented by gold borders upon mahogany, at the head of which is a grand looking-glass having above it the King's Coat of Arms in gold, and beneath a rich dressing table designed for Her Majesty. The other Royal apartments are embellished in a like manner. The two staircases are rich

The stately yacht Royal Caroline was among the perquisites to which England's George III succeeded in 1760. George renamed the yacht Royal Charlotte in honor of his bride-to-be, Princess Charlotte of Mecklenburg-Strelitz, and sent the vessel to bring the Princess to England. Welcomed aboard the lavishly appointed yacht, Charlotte asked: "And am I worthy of all these honors?"

beyond conception, the balustrades are of mahogany, richly carved and ornamented with gold."

A *Naval Chronicle* writer noted that *Royal Sovereign's* sailors were mildly sarcastic about her "abundance of gingerbread work," but another reporter proclaimed that *Royal Sovereign* was "the most perfect vessel of her class ever constructed."

One area that George III avoided with distaste during his yachting holidays was the popular south coast resort of Brighthelmstone. There, his brother the Duke of Cumberland, whom the King considered a wastrel, kept a summer house, spent large sums on a racing stable and frittered away his days hunting stag, gambling, drinking and overeating. George III discouraged his children from visiting Brighthelmstone. But in 1783 his eldest son, the Prince of Wales, turned 21 and headed straight for his uncle's seaside home.

The town was gaining popularity as a health spa, and young Prince George hoped the climate and waters would help relieve a case of swollen glands. He bought a farmhouse and commissioned a small palace, which he called the Marine Pavilion. He expanded this place over a period of 30 years until it was a hodgepodge of Gothic decorations, Indian-style apartments and stables ornamented with Chinese motifs. Sir Walter Scott, when he was visiting the area, pleaded, "Set fire to the Chinese stables, and if it embrace the whole of the Pavilion, it will rid me of a great eyesore."

George became Prince Regent in 1811 after his father was declared terminally insane; but he did not noticeably alter his pleasure-loving life style. Dissipation had made Prince George so grossly overweight that he could mount a horse only by being wheeled in his chair up a ramp and lowered by tackle onto the groaning animal. Understandably, he found yachting a more practical pastime, and in 1817 he took delivery of a pleasure craft even larger and more luxurious than his father's *Royal Sovereign*. The new yacht, *Royal George*, was 330 tons burden and 103 feet long. "The vessel is the most elegant ever seen," gushed an admirer at the yacht's launching. "Ornamental devices in abundance are placed in various parts, all highly gilt, and producing superb appearance." While cruising the waters south of England aboard *Royal George*, the Prince was enchanted by the Isle of Wight. He purchased a beach cottage at the resort of Cowes, which was becoming a sea-bathing rival to Brighton, and most of his recreational sailing thereafter was in the Solent.

But when he was crowned George IV upon his father's death in 1820, the new King demonstrated that he understood the use of a yacht for affairs of state as well as for pleasure. He decided to dramatize his role as ruler of all the United Kingdom by making visits to Ireland and to Scotland. These formerly independent lands had never completely reconciled themselves to English sovereignty.

On August 12, 1821—his 59th birthday—the King stepped off *Royal George* at Howth, a fishing village nine miles from Dublin. Wearing a blue coat and pantaloons, and sporting a blue cloth cap with a gold band, he plunged into a crowd of fishermen, shaking hands. As he drove to a royal lodge near the village, he was escorted by dozens of Irish farmers and gentlemen on horseback and thousands more on foot. He invited the

throng onto the grounds of the lodge, shook hands all around again and announced that this was "one of the happiest days of my life." Touring the area, he was met with ovations wherever he went; and in Dublin the Irish political leader Daniel O'Connell presented him with a laurel crown. When he reboarded *Royal George*, the shore was crowded for miles with his cheering Irish subjects.

Two years later George IV went to Scotland. As his yacht slipped into the ancient port of Leith, the rigging of every coaster and fishing boat swarmed with curious Scottish seamen, and the roofs of the waterfront homes and boarding houses were layered with townspeople. One of the first aboard *Royal George* to welcome the King to Scotland was his one-time Brighthelmstone neighbor Sir Walter Scott, who had returned to his native Edinburgh. Scott had been delegated to present George IV with a gift from the ladies of Edinburgh. The King and his hosts drank a toast of cherry brandy. Scott put his glass in his pocket as a memento of the occasion, but by the time he got home he had forgotten about it and sat on it, fortunately with more damage to the memento of the monarch than to the poet's posterior.

When the King stepped from the yacht onto a barge, cannon boomed and the crowds cheered. The barge was rowed to the landing, accompanied by a huge fleet of private boats, while warships and batteries ashore saluted. On the wharf the King was greeted by the skirls from a band of pipers. Royal archers and Scots Greys stood guard amid flowers and decorations. Three great cheers went up from the nearby shipyards. George IV, stuffed into an admiral's uniform and visibly moved by the drama that he had caused, advanced into a wave of officials and clergy bowing in greeting and subservience. The western and northern jewels in his crown were intact.

George IV is better remembered by yachtsmen for another gesture, made while he was Prince Regent. On September 15, 1817, when *Royal George* was anchored off Cowes, an aide to the Prince sent a note ashore to the members of a group called the Yacht Club: "SIR, The Prince Regent desires to be a member of the Yacht Club, and you are to consider this as an official notification of his Royal Highness's desire. I have the honour to be, sir, your obedient humble servant, Charles Paget."

The Prince Regent was welcomed by the members, who professed to be honored, but no doubt little realized the event's significance in the history of yachting. The seagoing sport of kings was no longer quite that. It had become so popular with lesser folk that royalty was stepping down into their ranks. Purple sails now seemed as ancient as Cleopatra.

In 1804 the largest and fastest royal English yacht yet built—a 96-foot three-master—was christened Royal Sovereign. Velvets, damasks, satins and mahogany paneling adorned her interiors, and the yacht's exterior was ornamented with gilded carvings. Here, with an honor guard of men-of-war, she takes Louis XVIII from exile in Britain to ascend the throne of France.

Chapter 2

Bastions of privilege ashore and afloat

Scottish and Irish members of one of Britain's earliest yacht clubs, the Royal Northern, rally at a Clyde regatta in 1825.

hat the British would invent the yacht club was almost inevitable. The very notion of clubs first manifested itself among the British; they originated as informal coffee-house gatherings in late-17th Century London. Joseph Addison, a noted social commentator of the day, defined the purpose of a club thusly: "Man is said to be a sociable animal, and, as an instance of it, we may observe that we take all occasions and pretences of forming ourselves into those little nocturnal assemblies, which are commonly known by the name of clubs." Selectivity in one's choice of companions was the organizing principle of such assemblies, and it obviously had application in many areas besides coffee drinking. Among the yachtsmen sailing around the British Isles, for example, the concept of selectivity was the most natural thing in the world. A club was their foreordained métier.

The earliest yachting association, which was formed in 1720, did not mention yachts in its name: It was called the Water Club of the Harbour of Cork. The club's founders came from the aristocracy and the gentry who lived in and around that ancient town on the south shore of Ireland. As members of the country's English ruling class, they were "delicately sensitive of any infringement of class or position," as one social historian politely put it.

They established the club's headquarters on an island in the harbor at Cork. Its name, Haulbowline, was suitably nautical, and it offered a satisfying measure of separation from the *hoi polloi* on shore. The club's membership was limited to 25, who were called captains, indicating that each member had his own yacht. No guests were permitted on the club premises "unless they should lie at the Captain's house the night before"—a system that effectively screened visitors, since no one of mean rank would be the house guest of a member. But on their island sanctuary the members permitted themselves a certain democracy in attire: A club rule forbade "long tail wigs, large sleeves, or ruffles"—marks of gentility in ordinary affairs.

Their yachting clothes may have been simple, but their sailing activities were not. Every two weeks from April through September, the Water Club captains sallied forth from their island to engage in elaborate processions and maneuvers that rivaled those of the Royal Navy. Disdaining racing, they preferred the challenge of sailing their vessels in parade and close-order drill. Their regattas reached a climax once each year when the Water Club flotilla, in stately line of battle and accompanied by nearly every good-sized boat in the harbor, sailed a few miles out into the Irish Sea to hold a grand annual review. This spectacle was described by a contemporary as being "like that of the Doge of Venice wedding the sea"—a reference to a magnificent annual procession that was intended to reaffirm Venice's age-old ties to the Adriatic. "The fleet," the same observer wrote to a nobleman friend, "is attended with a prodigious number of boats with their colours flying, drums beating, and trumpets sounding, and forms one of the most agreeable and splendid sights your lordship can conceive."

The Cork Water Club's yachts, judging by early paintings done of them by the celebrated marine artist Peter Monamy, were wide-beamed cut-

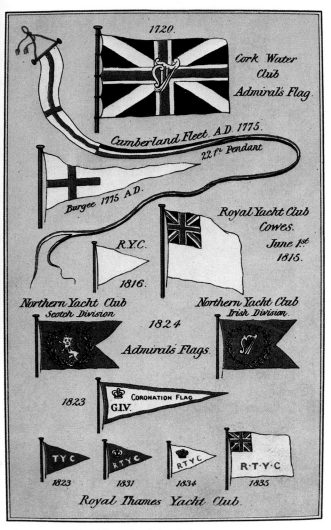

ters about 45 feet long, with bluff bows and lengthy bowsprits permitting a pair of jibs; their shape and rig were similar to that favored at the time for pilot boats and revenue cutters—as well as the smuggling vessels the cutters pursued. Because of their size, they provided only a moderate amount of cabin room, but they were splendidly suited for ceremony. The same observer who drew the Venetian parallel proudly noted that they were no ugly ducklings: "For painting and gilding, they exceed the King's yacht." Their club burgee was a " Union flag, with the Royal Irish Harp and Crown on a green field in the centre." Some of them had elaborately carved sterns and a few gunports; evidently the latter saw considerable use, since the members spent much of their time signaling to one another with their cannon. Part of the expense of the gunpowder was raised by levying fines against members who committed such offenses as missing or being late for these processions without a proper excuse.

Pomp and protocol were everything. The Water Club's top officers were given the titles of Admiral and Vice Admiral (even the club steward had the designation Knight of the Island of Haulbowline). The duties of the admiral were spelled out in meticulous detail—and so were his privileges: He alone was permitted to bring along any guests he wished. He administered the 27 rules and orders of the Water Club, and was grand marshal of the mock naval maneuvers. The firing of two guns and the hoisting of a white flag aboard his yacht brought the vice admiral hurrying alongside. To summon a captain, the admiral hoisted a pennant and fired "as many guns as the Captain is distanced from him and from the same side"; that is, if the admiral wanted the fifth yacht in the formation, he fired five guns.

The admiral's word was indeed law for the membership. One club rule read that "the Admiral singly, or any three captains whom he shall appoint, do decide all controversies or disputes that may arise at the Club, and any captain that shall refuse to abide by such decision, is to be expelled." Even the severity of a sailor's illness could be decided by the admiral: If a captain wanted to send a sick man ashore during a procession, he was first expected to signal a request for permission from the admiral; a white flag hoisted aboard the admiral's yacht granted permission, but a red flag meant that the procession could not be interrupted, and the sick man would have to wait.

For all the relentless dignity of their sailing style, the members of the club seem to have been a congenial, not to say bibulous, group. After holding their formal parades they came ashore on Haulbowline Island for what were considerably less formal dinners and drinking parties. The members took turns acting as host at these parties, in the order of their seniority. At dinner there were loud and lively discussions of the captains' performances during the maneuvers. In fact, so heated did these discussions tend to become that restraint had to be applied: A special rule ordered that anyone who "shall talk of sailing after dinner be fined a bumper" of wine.

The Water Club of the Harbour of Cork survived for 45 years, disbanding in 1765—and for a practical reason. Over the course of the next few decades, while England was at war with her former colonies in Amer-

The ensigns of British yacht clubs vied for colorful display. From the top: the Cork Water Club; a pennant used by the Cumberland Fleet surrounding the burgee of the same club; two insignia of the Royal Yacht Club (later the Royal Yacht Squadron); Scottish (left) and Irish divisions of the Northern Yacht Club; and two offshoots of the Cumberland Fleet: the Coronation Sailing Society, and four flags of the Royal Thames Yacht Club.

ica and with Napoleonic France, the waters around the British Isles were frequently unsafe.

The Thames, however, was free of enemy warships, and the organization credited with being the next yacht club was formed in London. Organized originally as a rowing club, it had increasingly attracted members—many with homes along the riverfront—who styled themselves as "very respectable gentlemen, proprietors of sailing vessels and pleasure boats." In 1775 these gentlemen formed the Cumberland Fleet, taking the name of their chief patron, the Duke of Cumberland. Their main pastime was sailing in procession on the river, although a few intrepid members ventured into Channel waters. In 1777, one yacht, *Hawke,* was chased by an American privateer, narrowly escaping into Calais, a harbor of neutral France.

The Duke of Cumberland died in 1790, but the club kept his name until 1823, at which point some of its members formed a new association, calling it the Thames Yacht Club. It was not, however, the first to signify its activity with the word "yacht" in its name. That distinction belongs to an organization that had begun its long and colorful existence eight years earlier.

A combination of circumstances gave birth to this remarkable institution. By 1815 the seas around the British Isles were relatively safe: Horatio Nelson had defeated the combined French and Spanish fleets at Trafalgar a decade earlier, and the wars with the Americans were nearly over. Meanwhile, social clubs had proliferated in England, growing increasingly specialized and exclusive.

In London, for example, the clergy were members of Child's, and the Jacobite politicians belonged to the Cocoa Tree. Women had their own club, Almack's, a set of rooms located on King Street where balls and suppers were given once a week during the social season. Almack's was rigidly exclusive itself and was dominated by London's current *grandes dames* of society. Men were admitted as guests only if they were good dancers—and only if they were attired in formal knee breeches; the Duke of Wellington was politely but firmly refused admittance when he showed up one evening wearing trousers.

More exclusive even than Almack's was White's, a men's club where the most notorious snobs and dandies in the city took their greatest pleasure in denying membership for whimsical reasons. The official history of the club would later admit that "the proceedings at the ballots became almost grotesque." Prospective members were refused for such reasons as wearing the wrong tie. Even Lord Castlereagh, the Foreign Secretary, was excluded.

For all their savage snobbery, members of the club tended to be sportsmen. One of them, Lord Grantham, proposed the formation of a sub-club, composed of White's members who were "interested in yachting." They met on June 1, 1815, at London's Thatched House Tavern, and promptly agreed upon an initiation fee of three pounds three shillings, and annual dues of two pounds two shillings. Membership was open only to owners of large yachts, with a burden of at least 10 tons. With grand simplicity, the founders called their organization The Yacht Club.

So rapid had been the revival of offshore yachting that 42 owners qualified and joined up. Titles were commonplace among the membership: There were two marquesses, three earls, four viscounts, four barons and five baronets. But the founders encouraged an atmosphere of informality, dispensing with officers. Nor did they feel an immediate need for a clubhouse; they agreed to meet twice a year, in the spring at the Thatched House Tavern and in summer at "the hotel at East Cowes" on the Isle of Wight.

The island, off the south coast of England, was so strategically located that it had been occupied by the Romans during the First Century A.D. and later had been fortified by the Normans and the British. By the time of the Yacht Club's founding, the Roman buildings were gone and only three of the British forts remained. But for the club members Cowes was a natural choice. The waters around the Isle of Wight provided an ideal area for cruising. The Solent and the Spithead, the western and eastern passages between the island and England's south coast, offered relatively protected water, and suitable anchorages were plentiful. Beyond lay the Channel and the ports of the Continent, which served as stepping-stones for cruises to the Mediterranean and the Riviera. Many of the club's members already had bought or built cottages on the island. Others spent their vacations, when they were not cruising, aboard their yachts at anchor off Cowes.

These pleasure craft were large and comfortably appointed; a Southampton reporter described them with tongue in cheek: "They have all the accommodation of a house, and are free from the inconvenience of a bad neighbourhood, for their site may be changed at pleasure; they have not only the richest, but also the most varied prospects; they are villas free from house duty and window tax; pay neither tithe nor poor rate; are exempt from government and parochial taxes; and have not only a command of wood and water, but may truly be said to possess the most extensive fishery of any house in England."

The founding members of The Yacht Club were less interested in racing than in cruising and in executing pseudonaval formation sailing of the kind that was favored by Cork's Water Club. On the first and third Mondays of each month in the summer, the yachtsmen brought their boats into line in Cowes Road for maneuvers under the direction of a commodore "appointed for the day." It was a pleasant, unpretentious pastime, and so inexpensive that in the second year of the club's existence the membership was able to suspend annual dues, making do with entrance fees alone.

This state of financial affairs changed, however, after His Royal Highness the Prince Regent requested membership in September of 1817, to be followed shortly by his younger brothers, the Duke of Clarence and the Duke of Gloucester. Annual dues were reinstated in 1818: They were needed to cover the costs of entertaining the eminent new members with proper banquets.

After the Prince Regent became King in 1820, the club added the prefix "Royal" to its name. George IV's first visit to Cowes after succeeding to the throne was a triumph. He sailed across the Solent to Cowes in *Royal George,* bowing to ladies who waved to him from the Southampton steamer. "He is not sparing of showing his person," a reporter wrote, "spending the greater part of the day on deck." Three Royal Yacht Club vessels sailed in the escorting flotilla.

Royal patronage was no small thing in a society so markedly hierarchical as that of 19th Century England. During succeeding decades, a number of yacht clubs throughout Britain attempted to attract royal attention and, in so doing, gain the social glory that had accrued to the yachtsmen of Cowes. The old Cumberland Fleet, now named the Thames Yacht Club, won from George IV's successor, William IV, permission to call itself the Royal Thames Yacht Club. At the opposite end of the kingdom, a quest for royal recognition was launched by a club whose membership defined itself as "certain gentlemen in the North of Ireland and the West of Scotland." This Northern Yacht Club, founded in 1824, was more formal than its southern counterparts, with a rigid dress code that fined members who did not appear at dinner attired in the prescribed blue, crimson-lined jacket, white or black pantaloons, or breeches and silk stockings. William IV granted the club the "Royal" prefix in 1830. And three years afterward he awarded the accolade to a yacht club that sprang up in Plymouth.

By that time, yacht clubs had appeared far beyond the British Isles. On the rocky peninsula at the entrance to the Mediterranean, a group of British Army and Navy officers founded the Gibraltar Yacht Club in 1829, the first of numerous such clubs that would be organized around the Empire (the Gibraltar Yacht Club did not earn its "Royal" designation until a century later). The craze spread to other European countries as well. A Royal Swedish Yacht Club came into being in 1830. In 1843, the son of French King Louis-Philippe, the Prince de Joinville, lent his royal support to the Société des Régates du Havre, an organization that had been put together five years earlier in an effort to promote a resort hotel located in Le Havre.

The Dutch, who could be credited with the birth of yachting two centuries earlier, did not have their first club until 1846, when Prince Hendrik (nicknamed The Seafarer) talked his father, King Willem II, into sponsoring the Royal Netherlands Yacht Club; the initial purpose of the club was to encourage rowing races, but sailing yachts were soon holding regattas in Rotterdam and Amsterdam. And an imperial yacht club was founded under the patronage of Czar Nicholas of Russia in the same year (some Russian yachting writers later claimed that the little flotilla of vessels assembled by Peter the Great in 1718 could be considered history's first yacht club; but this congregation of Peter's noble friends was hardly voluntary).

Nevertheless, yachting in Europe remained predominantly a British sport. As late as 1880, when there were 72 yacht clubs in Europe, more than half were British. While yacht racing had its ardent followers among the members of these clubs, most yacht owners preferred naval parades and processions.

George IV bore much of the credit for that, lending his presence to such spectacles throughout the years of his reign. In 1823, for example, he arranged for three of his own yachts to put on a dazzling show at Cowes. *Royal George, Royal Sovereign* and *Prince Regent,* on a signal, simultaneously got under way and sailed in formation down the shore-

Yachting on London's "silver flood"

The natural birthplace for British yachting was the broad River Thames, a "silver flood"—as Samuel Johnson put it—flowing through the heart of London. It was on the Thames that King Charles II, the first British yachtsman, sailed in his royal pleasure craft during the 1660s. Less than a century after that, the Italian artist Antonio Canaletto visited London and found the river reminiscent of Venice, where he had made his name painting the processions of royal barges on the Grand Canal. Canaletto proceeded to paint a series of panoramas—shown here and on the following pages—that highlighted the similarity between the two waterways.

Already the Thames was the arena of organized regattas of pleasure boats, which were usually held under royal patronage. Sometimes the yachts sailed 30 or so miles to the mouth of the river, where it is five and a half miles wide. The regattas attracted tens of thousands of shoreside spectators and were accompanied by flotillas of lesser vessels, some of them transporting musicians who serenaded the yachtsmen and their guests.

For another half century, while Britain warred with France and with her own American colonies, the Thames provided protection from enemy vessels in the Channel and the North Sea. The river thus remained the principal playground for what a contemporary termed the "fluviatic frolics" of Englishmen who sailed for sport. However, as soon as peace was restored in the early 19th Century, the more open waters of England's south coast—especially around the Isle of Wight—usurped the Thames's role as the center of British yachting.

With the dome of St. Paul's Cathedral in the background, ornate barges and boats traverse the Thames in a view by Canaletto from the north bank.

The long, stately barge of the Lord Mayor of London, in the foreground of this Canaletto painting, is rowed across the Thames below the just-completed Westminster Bridge on Lord Mayor's Day, 1747. Other flag-bedecked barges belong to the ancient city guilds, such as (from left in foreground) the skinners', the goldsmiths' and the fishmongers'. One reason for so much river activity was the scarcity of bridges across the Thames; this new span was London's first stone bridge in some 600 years.

A vessel believed to be a royal barge is moored below the Tower of London in a detail from a 1771 painting by Samuel Scott, an English marine artist. By now, riverscapes of the Thames were particularly popular with London's art patrons.

line. The *Southampton Herald* exclaimed: "It is impossible to describe the ecstasy with which they were seen moving gracefully through the immense fleet of vessels which covered the surface of these waters. Nor was this the completion of the treat; the squadron took a second time the same course, and after passing as close as possible to the shore, came once more to their respective berths. The effect which this unexpected and elegant manoeuvre produced was electric. From 8,000 to 10,000 persons witnessed it, and we will venture to say that the most fastidious observer will be ready to admit that at this point the highest expectations were perfectly consummated."

The following year, 19 Royal Yacht Club members took their procession all the way across the English Channel to Cherbourg, where they visited for three days. The *Southampton Herald* had patronizingly declared that their precision parades would be a "novel sight to the French nation, when they behold some of the finest vessels in the world." The French were indeed impressed—but not as impressed as the *Herald,* which also challenged any "watering-place in England to compete with Cowes or to produce a collection of such brilliant stars of fashion as at present illumine our hemisphere."

In 1825 the Royal Yacht Club finally established a headquarters, leasing a house on the Cowes waterfront. The expense that was entailed in setting up the first permanent clubhouse resulted in an increase in the annual dues, first to five pounds, then to eight pounds, and in raising the entrance fee to £10. The club also appointed its first fulltime commodore and adopted a uniform that has been standard yachting kit ever since: dark blue jacket, black four-in-hand tie and white trousers. A special white ensign was decreed for the members' yachts. It remained for George IV's openhanded successor, William IV, to give the Cowes club an even closer connection to the sovereign and the Royal Navy by designating it the Royal Yacht Squadron, and it has been called by this name ever since.

The royal presence had by this time transformed what had once been a casual yachting scene into a floating court. Members of the squadron sailed attendance on the King and Queen as they went from port to port around England to show themselves to their subjects, or headed across the English Channel to France on state visits. And in August 1826, the Royal Yacht Squadron staged a gathering of several days that would make Cowes even more the official center of yachting high society. The events consisted of an impressive regatta and a grand Regatta Ball; but the get-together—which was repeated every year thereafter, earning the appellation of "Cowes Week"—soon became known even more for its parties than for its seamanship.

A participant named Mrs. Nicholas Matthews Condy described the new scene: "A week at Cowes is pleasant enough, provided it is the Regatta week, and you have a sail every day, and do everything that is to be done in the way of gaiety; so we got on very well, between sails round the island, champagne luncheons, a very pleasant archery meeting at Carisbrooke, and a final wind up with the Royal Yacht Squadron Ball, unusually gay, and certainly the most amusing one at which I ever had the good fortune to be present."

The tradition of banquets and balls had actually begun in 1824, when Lord Yarborough celebrated the end of the summer season by giving a party for 300 guests on board his 71-foot brig *Falcon*. At 11 p.m. dancing started on deck. At two o'clock in the morning a champagne supper was served belowdecks. "On withdrawing from the banquet," reported the ever-present *Southampton Herald*, "dancing recommenced and was kept up with greatest spirit and enjoyment till four o'clock, when the boats assembled round the *Falcon* to convey the visitors to their respective homes; many of the boats were fitted up as gondolas, with lamps, and had a most pleasing appearance."

Two years after that, Yarborough had an even larger *Falcon* (102 feet), and was host to an even larger party, which set the *Herald* fairly quivering with ecstatic prose. "Between decks," the paper reported, tables were "covered with every delicacy of the season and the choicest wines." The interior of *Falcon* had been transformed with "festoons of evergreens" into a bower "resembling a natural grove, rendering the appearance of the supper cabins truly delightful. On deck," the correspondent continued, "waltzing and quadrilles were the order of the night; and never was that same frolicsome sylph, light-heeled Terpsichore, more devotedly worshipped or the buoyant bosom of old father Neptune more delightfully enchanted by a concord of sweet sounds. The graceful sport was kept up with unabated spirit, until the golden hue of morning's dawn broke through the gray-eyed twilight in the east." In other words, they danced until dawn.

Commodious and well-furnished yachts like *Falcon* were better suited to Cowes Week quadrilles and banquets than was the converted house that served as the squadron's spartan headquarters. In 1855, however, the members were presented with the opportunity to provide themselves with a more adequate clubhouse.

On the Parade, as Cowes's waterfront boulevard was called, squatted a compact castle that had given the town its name: Early castles were called *cowes*. It was the home of Lord Anglesey, one of the squadron's founders and the Governor of the island. After his death, the squadron took over his lease from the Crown and moved in. Originally built by Henry VIII in 1539 to defend the approaches to Southampton, the castle, with its stubby tower and low battlements, resembled a monastery from the waterfront, a nobleman's town house from the rear and, to some eyes, a prison from any angle. The building was in such disrepair that the squadron had to spend some £6,000 to make it usable. But its rooms and grounds were spacious enough to accommodate the largest parties, especially the Regatta Ball, which attracted the cream of British royalty and society to put a proper ending to Cowes Week.

The Prince Regent's Royal George, at anchor in Cowes Road (right), is the main attraction of the 1819 Cowes yachting season. In less than half a century royalty transformed the little village on the Isle of Wight (inset) from a yachtsmen's informal rendezvous into a central feature of England's summer social calendar.

There were a few veteran sailors who were repelled by the change in Cowes from the old days of simple sailing. One of the critics sneered: "The so-called yachtsmen of Cowes, it seems, have champagne lunches in the Solent, and then spread canvas and take a two hours' run when the breeze is fair and light. They meet the same people at Cowes as they meet later at the grouse"—he was referring, of course, to a grouse shoot—"and this life which they make to resemble Heaven must be a live facsimile of Hell. Different clothes and the same well-fed, carefully exercised bodies, the same bored minds tired of wondering whether passion will ever come their way."

By now, the Royal Yacht Squadron had become ultraexclusive. As with London clubs, the usual method for maintaining this exclusivity was the infamously capricious use of the blackball.

In the balloting method that was used by early London clubs, a mem-

ber voting on the admission of a proposed candidate dropped either a white ball (signifying approval) or a black ball (signifying disapproval) into a box; a stipulated number of black balls constituted rejection of the candidate. The Royal Yacht Squadron's voting procedure provided even greater secrecy. Each member of the squadron was given one cork ball, to be dropped in a mahogany box with a hole big enough to admit his hand. The box's interior had two drawers, a white one marked "yea" on the right and a black one marked "nay" on the left. The squadron member reached inside and dropped the cork ball into the right drawer for approval or the left to signify a blackball. After the voting was completed, the drawers of each compartment were inspected by the commodore to determine the results. By squadron rules, one negative vote in 10 was sufficient to doom a candidate's prospects.

In earlier years, the members of the Royal Yacht Squadron used the blackball sparingly and for generally understandable reasons. One applicant was denied admission because his yacht was such a sorry craft that she would have been an insult to the squadron's fleet. She was built "like a river barge with a flat bottom," said *Sporting Magazine*, and added, only partly in jest, that she was reported to have taken "two months in her voyage from the Thames to Cowes," a distance of 200 miles. Neither did many members object to the blackballing of Lord Cardigan in 1845. No yachtsman could excuse Cardigan's abysmal ignorance of the fundamentals of sailing. When asked by his captain one day if he would like to take the helm, Cardigan replied, " No, thank you, I never take anything between meals."

Presumably Cardigan found a way to correct his deficiencies, because the club finally accepted him as one of its members in 1848, and he thus was able to fly the Royal Yacht Squadron burgee on his yacht *Dryad* when it was anchored in Balaklava harbor in 1854 during the Crimean War. While his fellow officers lived in the tents with their men, Cardigan, a general, earned their displeasure by sleeping aboard his yacht and being served by his French chef.

Regrettably, as the squadron became more social than nautical, blackballs were cast for reasons of politics, spite or pure whimsy. Perhaps the most idiosyncratic example was that of a member who regularly blackballed anyone whose name began with the same initial as his. This policy ensured that he could tell at a glance whether he had any mail, since no other member would be using the slot that carried his initial in the club's letter rack.

One rejected candidate for membership rebelled openly. His real name was never recorded; a likely guess is that he was N. Power O'Shee, who owned the armed schooner *Daphne*. He was nicknamed "The Pirate" because some of the members believed that his yacht had 16 guns. The Pirate suspected Sir Percy Shelley, son of the poet, of being chiefly responsible for his being blackballed. True to his nickname, The Pirate anchored his schooner off the clubhouse and sent in a message that he would open fire if Shelley did not send him a letter of apology within the next half hour. It was dinnertime, and Shelley sat at his table, refusing to concede, while the other members watched him anxiously. Finally Sir Allen Young, who knew O'Shee well, convinced Shelley that it was no idle threat. Shelley grudgingly agreed to write the requested note. It was rushed out to the schooner; The Pirate dipped his ensign, weighed anchor and sailed off.

The Pirate was clearly volatile to excess, but the ranks of the Royal Yacht Squadron contained a number of men possessing an abundance of seafaring panache. Lord Belfast was one. Belfast ordered Joseph White, a Cowes shipwright, to build a yacht speedier than the Royal Navy's crack 10-gun brigs. The result, his *Waterwitch,* could outsail every Navy vessel of her size. Indeed, Belfast took a special delight in hovering near the naval base at Portsmouth, waiting for a ship to emerge; he would thereupon sail rings around the vessel. One day he came winging down on H.M.S. *Vestal,* then discovered that Princess Victoria was aboard; taking full advantage of the situation, he made a great display of shortening sail so as not to fly past a ship carrying a royal personage. Ultimately the Royal Navy purchased *Waterwitch* and copied her lines to produce new and swifter 10-gun brigs.

Another doughty squadron member found himself in the middle of one of the naval battles of the American Civil War. The Confederate commerce raider *Alabama,* which had been built in a British shipyard for the rebel navy, had cruised around the world, capturing 63 Union warships, merchantmen and whalers. Finally, on June 19, 1864, the Union man-of-war U.S.S. *Kearsarge,* which had been looking for the *Alabama* for months, caught up with her near Cherbourg. While the two warships were exchanging broadsides, British yachtsman John Lancaster stumbled on the scene in his *Deerhound.*

Instead of sailing clear of the 11-inch shells that were splashing around him, Lancaster moved into the battle zone in order to get a better view. So close did he get that, when the *Kearsarge's* superior gunnery sank the *Alabama,* the Confederate captain, Raphael Semmes, and some of his crew members were able to swim over to *Deerhound.* Lancaster hauled them aboard and then brought them into Cowes. Rushing to the clubhouse, he excitedly recounted his adventure. Lord Wilton, then commodore of the squadron, failed to recognize Lancaster as a fellow member, but felt he should do something for the bearer of this momentous news. He turned to his companion and whispered, "Do you suppose we should offer him a glass of sherry?"

Whether sedate or brimming with adventure, yachting required armies of servants and navies of seamen. In 1834 the Royal Yacht Squadron's members owned 101 yachts and employed 1,200 men to crew them. The key figure was the yacht's master—the subject of many a treatise. One expert of the day, William Cooper, recommended "an elderly, steady and strictly sober man." The best, he concluded, could be found among the oystermen of the Isle of Jersey or among the trawlermen of the Irish Sea, the Clyde or the North Sea. Experienced seamen like these, Cooper predicted, could make "a vessel talk."

So valuable were good masters that yacht owners engaged in a certain amount of poaching, luring away masters with promises of higher pay. A yachting writer named Arthur G. Bagot advised, however, that even if a capable man were hired the owner should designate himself as master, "whether he knows anything about navigation or not." The official master, Bagot pointed out, has complete control of the vessel and can legally "do what he likes with both ship and owner." It was not "a pleasant experience," Bagot reminded his fellow yachtsmen, "to be ordered about by one's own servant."

The attire of officers was hardly less important than their skill, since—as yachtsman Cooper explained—"outward appearance has some little to do, as well as mental qualifications, in commanding respect." Cooper recommended that the master be outfitted in a "suit of blue cloth," as well as one of rougher material "for wet and cold weather." His blue dress cap might have "a gold band," and his suit jacket could be ornamented with the buttons of the owner's club. The yacht owner should be certain, however, to restrict the buttons to "the small waistcoast size," Cooper warned; "above all things avoid a display of 'gingerbread trappings.'"

The seamen, he said, should be dressed in "pilot cloth pea jackets, trowsers of the same material, and blue woollen shirts with rolling collars, loose bodies, and sleeves gathered into pleats at the wrists." Jaunty straw hats added the right note: "the light reflected from the straw gives a man's face a bright, cheerful expression." The sailors' hats should have black ribbons with the name of the yacht inscribed on them "in plain shaped, moderate sized, gilt letters." A set of oilskins and a sou'wester (a waterproof hat named for the powerful storms that blew in from the southwest) were essential to keep the crew member dry and warm. For "unless a man's bodily comfort is attended to," Cooper cautioned, "you cannot reasonably expect him to be cheerful and contented."

Bagot took another view of this matter, however. "Yacht hands will grumble at anything," he wrote, "but when they find it is no use, they soon turn the other way, and take a pride in carrying out the rules of the vessel. Believe me, therefore, at the root of everything, comfort, economy, and safety, lies that one word which has made England what she is, viz. Discipline."

Cooper proposed a routine that gives a fair idea of a crewman's life aboard a British yacht in the 19th Century. The men should be wakened early. Then, he advised, "let the decks be washed down the first thing, the gratings scrubbed, the bulwarks washed, the copper scoured, brasses cleaned and polished, running gear overhauled and made hand taut, ropes all coiled away in their proper places, water and coke, or other fuel got on board, hammocks and bedding stowed away, the forecastle scoured and cleaned out, and the galley fire lit, the boats washed out and overhauled, their oars, thole pins or crutches, rudders, yokes and lines, and respective boat-hooks laid ready for use." All of this should be completed by 8 a.m. Then and only then should the crew be permitted to wash and have their breakfast. Presumably men who had put in nearly a full day's work before breakfast would have little inclination—or strength—to complain.

The secretary of the Royal Yacht Squadron maintained a private blacklist of yacht hands who had been insubordinate or had committed some other misdeed: No one whose name was on this list could expect to be hired aboard another member's yacht. In 1869, however, the blacklist

A commodore too true to his club

LORD ALFRED PAGET

Few yachtsmen were more clearly born to the afterdeck than Lord Alfred Paget. Son of a founder of the Royal Yacht Squadron, Paget cut so dashing a figure that he stirred romantic sentiments in 18-year-old Queen Victoria. The Queen told a confidant, however, that "it would never do" to marry one of her subjects, regardless of his lineage.

In 1844, Paget's club, the Royal Thames, honored him with a citation (opposite) for "the distinguished services rendered by him on all occasions." In 1846 he was elected commodore—a post he held until 1873, when he stepped down so that Victoria's son Edward, Prince of Wales, could assume the office.

But he was willing to oblige the Queen only up to a point. When one of her yacht tenders, the *Alberta*, rammed and sank a schooner owned by a member of the Royal Thames, Paget supported his club's claim that the *Alberta* had been at fault. Victoria, evidently expecting perfect fealty in the matter, expressed great annoyance at Paget, but officials investigating the incident had the last word: the *Alberta*'s skipper had indeed "made an error of judgment."

A Royal Thames scroll honored Paget for his sailing expertise as well as for his "urbanity and hospitality to the members."

was dispensed with as possibly libelous—a danger that was pointed out by Sir Alexander Cockburn, a Royal Yacht Squadron member who was Britain's Lord Chief Justice.

Regardless of how assiduously owners tried to run their yachts according to Navy fashion, some missteps were bound to occur. These were all the more galling, of course, when there were guests aboard to witness them. As for the guests, their tendency was to react with barely suppressed amusement. Such, certainly, was the case with Mrs. Nicholas Condy on the occasion when she went for a Cowes Week cruise in 1843 aboard J. H.W.P. Smith-Pigott's 70-foot yacht *Ganymede*. Mrs. Condy described the experience in a pamphlet titled "Reminiscences of a Yachting Cruise," which must have assured her of receiving no further invitations from J. H.W.P. Smith-Pigott.

Her arrival provided a hint of what was to come. She was piped aboard in impressive naval style, with two side boys at the gangway, but the effect was spoiled by a bugler on deck who proceeded to salute her off-key. At the signal from the club's flagship *Kestrel*, the yachts paraded out into the Solent, whereupon the cook presented himself on *Ganymede's* quarter-deck to report that all the clean laundry had been left ashore. A wrathful Smith-Pigott signaled the flagship, requesting permission to "part company" with the fleet. This was distinctly bad form, but the embarrassment of returning was preferable to the humiliation of not being able to change the guests' sheets.

Riding a fair tide, *Ganymede* made good time on this misbegotten mission and rejoined the rest of the squadron yachts in time for dinner—and also in time for a freshening breeze that set all the yachts rolling heavily at anchor. When the guests had dressed and assembled in the dining saloon, they found that the dinner table was swinging from one side to the other on its gimbals. Mrs. Condy, unaccustomed to dining under such conditions, committed the *faux pas* of grabbing the edge of the table and stabbing at her plate before it swung away. Smith-Pigott barked at her, "Let go! Let go!," in fear that the next roll of the yacht would send everything cascading from the table onto the guests' laps: Glasses already were toppling from the dining saloon's stationary sideboard. Mrs. Condy resigned herself to dining "in a most decidedly uncomfortable manner," with her dinner and wine alternately appearing at chin height and swinging out of reach.

The wind increased and *Ganymede* rolled even more steeply. Finally the ladies gave up and stumbled to the main cabin, where they tried to preserve their decorum while they rocked back and forth. Mrs. Condy soon left and retired to her stateroom, but also could not get to sleep. Not only did she have to hold on to keep from being rolled off her bed; she was also kept awake by sounds that, "between the howlings of the storm, assumed a most frightful character"—an assortment of croaks, screeches and gurgles.

She climbed out of bed, struggled into her dressing gown with one arm while holding on with the other to keep from being tumbled the length of the stateroom, and went in search of an explanation. In the corridor she was joined by other equally impatient guests. They found the coxswain, who promptly explained: "Lord love ye, ladies, it's only

Sheet music for waltzes became almost as important as sailing directions when royalty transformed Cowes Week from a plain sailor's regatta to a floating social season in the early 19th Century. The waltzes in this book were composed especially for balls aboard the yachts of members of the Royal Yacht Squadron.

the fowls." The chickens brought along to provide fresh food were caged on deck near Mrs. Condy's stateroom. The coxswain added: "That bless'd old cock never will let any poor devil sleep after two o'clock, and the young un's larnin'!"

The next night, one of the gentleman guests, taking pity on Mrs. Condy in her plight, came up with an imaginative solution to the problem of the chickens: He attempted to anesthetize the birds by sneaking a ration of gin into their feed. "I am grieved to say," Mrs. Condy reported, "the experiment failed of its desired effect; for the creatures awoke next morning like 'giants refreshed,' an hour earlier than usual, crowing with renewed vigour."

Not even church services, it developed, could be held without misadventure during this unfortunate cruise. On Sunday morning, as the services began, a breeze filling the mainsail set *Ganymede* rolling and lurching. Unfazed, Smith-Pigott began reading a prayer for all at sea, "*particularly* the Royal Yacht Squadron." The breeze became gusty. "Flap went the mainsail," Mrs. Condy reported, "creak went the boom," knocking a French cabin boy named Antoine against the captain, whose hat flew overboard. Antoine swore, the captain cursed, the rooster crowed and the hens cackled. Struggling to keep her dignity, Mrs. Condy watched Smith-Pigott, whose "mixture of contending feelings displayed, when he found all his efforts to restore order ineffectual, gave him such a truly ludicrous appearance, that I was obliged to laugh in spite of myself. This," she wrote delicately, "put the finishing touch to the matter." The boatswain was meanwhile punctuating the service on his pipe. Finally Smith-Pigott bellowed: "Boatswain! pipe down and be damned!" The boatswain, Mrs. Condy gleefully recorded, responded with "a very solemn 'Amen!' Thus ended the first and last morning service."

Clearly, Smith-Pigott was not amused by this comic-opera cruise. To some Royal Yacht Squadron members, yachting was still a serious business. But the same comfort-loving trend that had altered the activities at Cowes from simple sailing to a series of balls and banquets was also having its effect on the yachts themselves. By the second half of the 19th Century, sail was giving way to steam.

The idea of mechanically propelled vessels was an ancient one. The Romans evidently had boats with paddle wheels turned by oxen on treadmills, and Chinese histories record man-powered paddle wheels in the Seventh Century A.D. Steam was seriously considered as a source of nautical propulsion as early as the 17th Century, but no practical steam vessels were built until the end of the next century. Thereafter, progress was rapid. In 1801, William Symington of Scotland built what was probably the first commercially successful steam-driven vessel, a tugboat used on canals in Great Britain.

Six years later, Robert Fulton launched the 150-foot steamboat *Clermont,* also known as the *North River,* and chugged up the Hudson River from New York City to Albany, a 150-mile journey completed in 32 hours. This achievement earned Fulton enormous popular acclaim and the title of inventor of the steamboat—in spite of the fact that he had built on the work of many others, and that the engine he used had been made in an English factory.

In the years immediately following, steamboats improved rapidly. But not until 12 years after Fulton's ride up the Hudson was a transatlantic steamship voyage attempted. The American vessel *Savannah* was in fact a full-rigged ship, fitted with a modest-sized steam engine of about 75 horsepower and folding paddle wheels that were stowed on deck during stormy weather. It took *Savannah* 29 days, 11 hours to sail from her home port of Savannah, Georgia, to Liverpool, and her steam power was used for only 85 hours of the voyage. Although she traveled onward from England to Russia, she failed to impress shippers as a reliable alternative to sail; she was stripped of her engines and finished her career as a conventional wind-powered vessel. But steam power was not to be denied. In 1838, two vessels, *Sirius* and *Great Western*, crossed the Atlantic solely under steam, completing their pioneering passages within a few hours of each other.

Yachtsmen had been watching the arrival of steam power with mixed emotions. The more adventurous among the owners began to consider the possibility of using steam for their yachts, but others responded with the slogan: Steam destroys seamanship. In 1827 the Royal Yacht Squadron came down firmly on the antisteam side of the argument: The membership passed a resolution stating that "as a material object of this club is to promote seamanship and the improvement of sailing vessels, to which the application of steam-engines is inimical, no vessel propelled by steam shall be admitted into the club and any member applying a steam-engine to his yacht shall be disqualified thereby and cease to be a member."

But as Mrs. Condy had discovered, sailing and comfort did not necessarily go hand in hand. A steam-powered yacht did not have to tack upwind, heeling in the process. Moreover, a steam yacht could be larger. For those owners to whom elegance at anchor was important, steam was clearly preferable—and some yachtsmen were determined to have it at any price. Two years after the Royal Yacht Squadron passed its anti-steam ordinance, a member named Thomas Assheton-Smith made the ultimate sacrifice: He resigned his membership in the squadron in order to commission the first British steam yacht on record, a 120-footer. Assheton-Smith had previously built five sailing yachts; henceforth, steam was to be his only interest. He would own eight steam yachts during his lifetime.

Steam yachts soon attracted a more formidable supporter: Queen Victoria. Her Majesty was persuaded of the merits of steam during her first official voyage—aboard a sailing yacht. She inherited *Royal George* from her uncle William IV, and in the summer of 1842 she used the royal yacht for a visit to Scotland. The 400-mile voyage from Woolwich to Leith took three days. The winds were fickle, and the Queen was not amused at the sight of passenger steamers plowing past while *Royal George's* sails slatted in the calm. To make her schedule, two paddle-wheelers were summoned to take *Royal George* in tow. "We heard, to our great distress, that we had only gone 58 miles since eight o'clock last night," Victoria wrote sourly in her diary. " How annoying and

Victoria's paddle-wheel palaces

No one liked the comforts of home afloat more than England's Queen Victoria did. The Queen was laid low by rough weather, and her husband, Prince Albert, was said to grow "pale and queasy the moment he spied a ship." But Victoria and her prince consort realized that a royal yacht was the most efficient way to show themselves to their subjects. So when in 1843 the royal couple commissioned a 225-foot paddle-wheeler named *Victoria and Albert,* they made certain that she resembled the sort of living quarters they enjoyed ashore.

Aboard this yacht *(below)* the Queen and her consort visited British ports as well as France and Portugal. But by 1855 their first yacht had been succeeded by *Victoria and Albert II,* partly because the Royal Family had grown to include nine children; *Victoria and Albert II* was 75 feet longer than her predecessor.

As the pictures on the following pages illustrate, the interiors of Victoria's second royal yacht were designed—largely by her husband—to combine comfort with ceremony. The reception rooms were regal rather than opulent, and the royal cabins were more livable than lavish. *Victoria and Albert II's* crew reflected the atmosphere that was appealing to the Queen.

Royal Navy seamen were selected for special abilities. Spoken orders were kept to a minimum; unnecessary noise was further reduced by the seamen's wearing rubber-soled shoes. Officers too were carefully chosen, and they enjoyed the distinction of this special duty. But after a long period of service, some were promoted to the command of Navy vessels. Victoria promptly stopped this practice. "I am an old woman," she complained, "and I like to see faces I know about me, and not have to begin with new faces."

From the paddle wheel of Victoria and Albert I, the Queen, Prince Albert and Prince Edward accept subjects' cheers in Plymouth in 1843.

The Queen's bedroom (top) aboard
Victoria and Albert II had steps to assist
the diminutive monarch into her bed.
A connecting door led to her husband's
dressing room (above), which was
equipped with a desk and maps on rollers.
The many windows of the dining room
(right) helped to counter the heaviness of
the leather-covered furniture.

A favorite retreat aboard her second yacht was the Queen's drawing room, with its deep sofa, a piano, a writing table and wall maps on rollers.

Victoria and Albert II's aft saloon was suitable for informal royal receptions. Couches lined the curved stern, and a porcelain stove warmed the room.

provoking this is! We remained on deck all day lying on sofas; the sea was very rough towards evening, and I was very ill." She insisted on chartering a steamer for the return trip and ordered a steam yacht as soon as she reached home.

The keel of the new yacht was laid that autumn; by spring the vessel was launched and christened *Victoria and Albert*. She was a 225-foot paddle-wheeler, with a drawing room suitably impressive for state receptions—nearly 25 feet long, 13 feet wide and painted a lilac color bordered with gold beading. Queen Victoria immediately put her floating plaything to practical use by cruising with her consort, Prince Albert, to port towns all around the British Isles. Thousands of people who had never expected to see their sovereign flocked to welcome her in such places as the Channel Islands, Wales and along the coast of Scotland as far north as the Caledonian Canal. *Victoria and Albert* also put into Plymouth and Penzance, Dartmouth and the Scilly Isles, making the royal presence available to more of the Queen's subjects than any of her predecessors had.

Victoria occasionally made voyages to France and Belgium in *Victoria and Albert*. But her most significant port of call was Cowes, where she and Prince Albert had fallen in love with a small Georgian mansion called Osborne House, which was owned by Lady Isabella Blachford. In 1845 the royal couple bought the house, and in the succeeding years they enlarged it, spending more and more of their time there. Albert laid out the formal gardens, and Victoria enjoyed the vistas across the sloping lawns to the sea.

Given the fact that Victoria, as Queen, was listed as the only woman member of the Royal Yacht Squadron, there could be no question of maintaining the ban on steam. By 1843, squadron members were joking about the subject: A resolution passed that year ordered "that steamers belonging to the Squadron shall consume their own smoke." But the members were merely surrendering gracefully. The following year, steam yachts whose engines exceeded 100 horsepower were deemed admissible—anything smaller was still beneath contempt. By 1853, however, all restrictions on steamers were lifted; steam was finally welcomed to the Royal Yacht Squadron.

By Victoria's standards, life at Osborne House and on board her yacht was roughing it. "The sailor-gypsy life we lead is *very* delightful," she wrote in her journal. Aboard *Victoria and Albert* the usually regal woman could unbend, however slightly. One day, in a freshening breeze that would have put a sailing yacht over on her side but merely made the steamer's deck windy, Victoria and two of her ladies-in-waiting sheltered themselves in the lee of a paddle-wheel box. The Queen, who missed nothing, noticed that the deck hands were gathering in small groups and whispering to one another. She sent for an officer and asked what the trouble was. He apologetically informed her that the day's ration of grog for the crew was stowed in a locker that she had inadvertently blocked with her deck chair. To the delight of the crew, the Queen agreed to move her chair on condition that she be allowed to join the men in a round. On tasting the grog, she announced that it "would be very good if it were stronger."

Victoria made at least 20 voyages aboard her royal yacht; and so pleased was she that in 1855 she requested a larger one. *Victoria and Albert II (pages 64-66)* was 300 feet long, a third again as large as her predecessor; she could make 15 knots, nearly four knots faster. And she was a paddle-wheeler, even though the screw propeller was by then becoming more popular.

The decision to build a paddle-wheeler had not been made lightly. The screw propeller, although more efficient, could cause a great deal of vibration. So Commander W. Crispin, second-in-command of the first *Victoria and Albert,* made a lengthy voyage aboard a screw-driven steamer in order to assess its performance. He concluded, "and very reluctantly so—from all my well-known predilections in favor of the Screw generally speaking over the Paddle," that a propeller-driven yacht "will in that vital & all important point—the personal comfort of Her Majesty, prove a total failure."

The interior decoration of the yacht was supervised by Prince Albert, who evidently liked the color green. Heavy green curtains hung in the corridors of the royal apartments; the Queen's bedroom was furnished with a mahogany bed canopied with rosebud chintz that was lined with green silk; green silk blinds and white muslin curtains covered the windows. The royal couple provided well for their attendants: The ladies-in-waiting had their own dining room, and there were 12 special cabins for 18 royal servants. The crew required for this floating palace numbered 240 officers and men.

Because *Victoria and Albert II* drew 16 feet, she needed tenders. The 161-foot tender *Fairy*, with a draft of only seven feet four inches, was able to take the Queen into waters where the deeper-draft yachts could not go: During a state visit to Amsterdam, for example, the royal couple went aboard the *Fairy* for a cruise through the shallow Scheldt. Another tender, the *Elfin*, with a draft of 4 feet 10 inches, carried the Queen's dispatches to shore from *Victoria and Albert II* and to the mainland from Osborne House, making the run on such a regular daily schedule that she was locally called the "milk boat." A third tender, the *Alberta,* was commissioned to carry Queen Victoria herself to and from the Osborne House pier at East Cowes. The *Alberta* was a paddle-wheeler, and she was beamy enough not to roll too much for the Queen's comfort. "Lack of motion is all important," cautioned Colonel Charles Phipps, who as Keeper of the Privy Purse commissioned the vessel. Her Majesty, he explained, "takes days to recover" from seasickness. "Speed is to be sacrificed if necessary" to avoid this discomfort.

The *Alberta* turned out to be a controversial craft, occasioning a bitter dispute between the First Lord of the Admiralty (the Royal Navy supervised the construction of royal yachts) and Prince Ernest of Leiningen, who was captain of *Victoria and Albert II* and also the Queen's nephew. The Prince went aboard the new tender and pronounced her "the greatest beast ever floated." He claimed that the paddle wheels shook the 160-foot *Alberta* so violently that Her Majesty "would have been frightened." Evidently Prince Ernest was being over-solicitous, because only minor alterations had to be made to the *Alberta,* supervised by Commander David N. Welch (as captain of the tender *Fairy* he had become expert at predicting what would and what would not bother the Queen).

Victoria's pleasure in yachting was grievously diminished after her beloved Prince Albert died in 1861. She became a near-recluse, and six years passed before she was again making ceremonial appearances aboard *Victoria and Albert II:* She attended a naval review at Spithead; and she chose the royal yacht for a formal investiture of the Order of the Garter on the Sultan of Turkey. But by then her example had already helped the steam yacht come of age.

Steamers still were vastly outnumbered: In 1863, for example, there were 30 steam yachts registered in England, compared with almost 800 sailing yachts. But many of the latter were outfitted with auxiliary steam engines, permitting their owners to cruise to the far harbors of the world. And the popularity of steam grew so rapidly that a decade later there were 140 British yachts powered by steam; 10 years after that, there would be 466. The steam yacht would continue to gain ascendancy—and become ever more luxurious—through the end of the century, until the coal-fired steam engine was replaced in the 20th Century by the more efficient engine powered by diesel oil.

On the quarter-deck of her yacht Victoria and Albert II, Queen Victoria (center), still in mourning for her husband six years after his death, bestows the Order of the Garter on the Sultan of Turkey (kneeling). There was a heavy swell in the Solent, and the Sultan was even queasier than the Queen.

Grand opening at Suez

Never had there been so grand a congregation of royal and private yachts; indeed, few such flotillas of any kind had ever assembled in peacetime. Lying at anchor in the harbor of Port Said, Egypt, were some 80 pleasure craft and warships that had gathered to celebrate the opening of the Suez Canal in 1869.

The spectacle began on November 16—and on land. In gilded, red-carpeted pavilions on Port Said's shore, the royal guests took part in the first large Moslem-Christian ceremony ever held (right). The next day, the yachts and warships paraded into the man-made waterway (pages 74-75) for the 100-mile passage to the Red Sea. The yacht of honor was the 160-foot black paddle-wheel steamer L'Aigle; it carried France's Empress Eugénie (inset, top right), whose husband, Napoleon III, had been the canal's chief supporter but had remained home in Paris. Also aboard L'Aigle was the Empress' cousin Ferdinand de Lesseps (inset, bottom left), designer and builder of the canal.

The largest yacht, Greif, belonged to Austrian Emperor Franz Josef (inset, upper left). Crown Prince Frederick of Prussia, Prince William Henry of Holland and Grand Duke Michael of Russia all had brought their own yachts. The host, Egypt's Khedive Ismail Pasha (inset, lower right), welcomed his guests aboard his Mahroussa, while around the royal vessels swarmed tourist-jammed steamers and the pleasure craft of ambassadors and aristocrats.

The yachts presented a symptomatic as well as dramatic sight: All but the smallest craft moved into the waterway under steam or tow and with sails furled. The Suez Canal, too narrow for a large sailing vessel to tack against head winds, provided a new shortcut to the East only for merchantmen or yachts powered by steam.

In a pavilion at Port Said, white-gowned Empress Eugénie (far right), flanked by Franz Josef of Austria on her right and Egypt's Khedive, watches as Moslem (left) and Christian (left center) hierarchies gather to mark the opening of the Suez Canal. Insets show the major participants; from top left, clockwise, Franz Josef, Eugénie, Khedive Ismail Pasha, and the designer of the canal, Ferdinand de Lesseps.

The Austrian paddle-wheeler Greif
joins other royal yachts (below) entering
the Suez Canal. Inset: a canopied,
multioared tender heads out to its yacht.

Empress Eugénie embarks on a steam
launch to go out to her yacht L'Aigle.
Thousands of Arabs had flocked to the
canal to witness the spectacle.

The banks of the Suez Canal were a panorama of the East—Arab tribesmen, pith-helmeted British India Army officers, turbaned Nile farmers, Circassian warriors—as the procession of royal yachts moved through the new waterway, led by Eugénie's *L'Aigle (right)*. Halfway along the canal, a new town, named after the Khedive, had sprung up. Ismailia bulged with 40,000 revelers. Dancers, magicians, jugglers and prostitutes swarmed through the town's narrow streets. And on the shores of the adjacent Lake Timsah, 30,000 invited nomads camped with their camels and feasted on barbecued sheep.

After a carefully escorted excursion into the desert, the royal guests assembled, along with several thousand other dignitaries, in the Khedive's new palace, specially constructed for the celebration and decorated, in the Empress' honor, in the style of France's Second Empire. Next morning, November 19, the royal yachts and their escorts moved down the remaining 45 miles of the canal to the port of Suez and the Red Sea. Aboard *L'Aigle*, Eugénie finally returned through the canal to the Mediterranean and steamed home to France. Thirty years later in her memoirs she was nostalgic about the "dreamlike resplendence" of the procession she had led to inaugurate a new age of maritime history.

Empress Eugénie's flag-dressed yacht, followed by an Egyptian escort, leads the way through the canal. Inset right: At the climactic banquet given by the Khedive (far right, wearing fez), Emperor Franz Josef is third from left, with Empress Eugénie on his left. The banquet included 24 courses and lasted into the early morning hours. The Khedive's party cost him the equivalent of more than seven million dollars.

On a side trip to the desert outside
Ismailia (inset), Eugénie and Franz Josef
ride in the lead carriage (center)
escorted by the Khedive at right.

Chapter 3

A Yankee flair for opulence

Salem's Crowninshield Wharf is lined in 1806 with ships that made the family rich and were prototypes of early U.S. luxury yachts.

t is a curious coincidence of history that yachting was introduced to America, as to England, by the Dutch. The first pleasure craft in North America were *jaght schips* sailed about the harbor of New Amsterdam by wealthy Dutch settlers in the early 17th Century; except in decorative elaboration, they differed little from the sprightly, cannon-carrying vessels that would attract the attention of England's exiled King Charles II in Amsterdam a few decades later.

The English continued to practice the sport on a modest scale after evicting the Dutch from America's Atlantic seaboard in 1664, but not much is known of their yachts. One anonymous 18th Century vessel is described only as having damask curtains at her portholes. Another pleasure craft was immortalized in a print of New York Harbor *(opposite)*; she was Colonel Lewis Morris' nimble little sloop *Fancy*, and was the most admired pleasure craft of the time.

In the 19th Century, however, luxury yachting in the New World would come into its own. Three men would dominate the scene. The pioneer of the pastime was George Crowninshield Jr., a romantic gadabout with more money than he could spend. Crowninshield's example was followed by a prototypical United States capitalist, Cornelius Vanderbilt, who turned to yachting—and to a trend-setting steamer—to enjoy his enormous, if sometimes ill-gotten, wealth. The supreme example of self-indulgence, however, was a colorful yachtsman named James Gordon Bennett Jr., who managed to squander a vast fortune on three floating palaces of pleasure. By their dedication to seaborne luxury, these three rapidly brought American yachting to the point where it was capable of holding its own against the most opulent efforts of the Old World. And in the process, they established a tradition that would lead to an even more lavish display by succeeding yachtsmen at the turn of the century.

America's first true luxury yacht was launched on October 21, 1816, in an unlikely port, Salem, Massachusetts, known principally for witch-hunters and tight-fisted merchants. Her name—*Cleopatra's Barge*—reflected a strong streak of romanticism in her owner, George Crowninshield Jr., an equally unlikely product of a hard-working, eminently serious-minded New England family. In a sense, he was a throwback. His great-grandfather had arrived in Boston in 1684, claiming to be a doctor of noble birth, Johann Kaspar Richter von Kroninschilt by name. It was rumored that he had left Europe because of gambling debts and even that he had killed a man in a duel. He practiced medicine and died penniless in 1711, leaving five children. His son John became a merchant—a profession that, at a time when Britain tried to maintain tight control over colonial trade through a series of laws known as the Navigation Acts, usually involved a good deal of smuggling. By his energetic activities on both sides of the law, John established the foundation of the family fortune; he also anglicized the immigrant doctor's name to Crowninshield. And John's son George built the family business into a mercantile empire.

George Crowninshield Sr., father of the future owner of *Cleopatra's Barge*, was a shining example of the maritime vigor of the new United

One of the earliest American pleasure craft, Colonel Lewis Morris' yacht Fancy (lower right), skims across New York Harbor while anchored vessels salute her in a 1717 engraving that shows the scene from the Brooklyn shore.

States. By 1805 his fleet numbered 12 vessels, trading as far afield as Sumatra, China and India. "Salem rolls in riches with every tide," wrote one member of the family firm. Although the big cities of Boston and New York had larger merchant fleets, Salem attained the highest per capita income of any town in the United States. The port's new-rich merchants built neoclassical mansions and furnished them with exotic artifacts from the East—cloisonné screens and inlaid tables, delicate china and silver swords.

Five Crowninshield sons served aboard the family's vessels, and all were captains by the age of 20. Two of them went on into politics, Jacob winning a seat in Congress and Benjamin being appointed Secretary of the Navy under Presidents Madison and Monroe. The Crowninshields had become the epitome of respectability—with the sole exception of George Jr., the eldest son.

A confirmed bachelor, George spent two decades at sea, then took up duties in the Crowninshield countinghouse, where he cut a most unusual figure. Only 5 feet 6 inches tall, he emphasized his rotund shape by disdaining the customary business suit that was worn by the Salem shipowners and attiring himself in colorful clothes made to his own design: an appliquéd waistcoat, knee breeches and gold-tasseled Hessian boots, with a high-crowned beaver-skin hat perched jauntily over his hair, which he tied in a pigtail. In place of the usual horse and buggy, George Jr. sped down to Salem's wharves in a bright yellow curricle drawn by two high-stepping horses.

Yet George Crowninshield was a shrewd, methodical logistician who carefully supervised the fitting-out of all Crowninshield ships. And for all his foppishness, he won Salem's respect as a man of action who seemed always to be first on the scene when help was needed; with no thought for his own safety, he rescued several people from burning buildings and on three occasions leaped into the water to save seamen from drowning. In 1801 the Massachusetts Humane Society awarded him its gold medal for heroism.

That same year he launched his first yacht. *Jefferson* was no luxury craft compared with what was to come, but she was remarkably fast for a 36-foot sloop. When the War of 1812 broke out, George sent *Jefferson* to sea as a privateer, her deck crowded with cannon and her hull jammed with 26 seamen. She promptly proved her speed, capturing three British schooners; their cargoes brought nearly $3,200, which by custom was split between the owner and the crew. During the War, five larger ships of the family fleet ran down 85 British merchantmen; one Crowninshield vessel, the brig *America IV*, took a series of prizes worth more than one million dollars. The Crowninshield family's profit from the War of 1812 was an estimated two million dollars, worth about $20 million in today's currency. George Sr. died in 1815 at the age of 81. His sons liquidated the firm and sold all the ships. George Jr., then 49 years old, was left boatless, restless and exceedingly rich.

To amuse himself, he traveled down the Mississippi and through the wilds of Kentucky. But inland America bored him. He returned home and went to Salem's most successful shipbuilder, Retire Becket, whose yard had produced the racing yacht *America IV*. There, he ordered a

George Crowninshield Jr. is smugly nautical in this 1816 portrait by Samuel F. B. Morse. Besides the telescope in Crowninshield's hand, Morse added his yacht Cleopatra's Barge under full sail in the background.

Running before a brisk breeze in a contemporary painting, Cleopatra's Barge displays her elaborate stern and the herringbone decoration on her port side. Owner Crowninshield whimsically ordered a contrasting pattern of horizontal stripes on her starboard side.

yacht that would be the fastest, sturdiest and most comfortable floating home yet built in America, and never mind the cost.

As the yacht took shape, George made periodic visits to the Becket shipyard to admire her on her ways, sometimes filling his carriage with inquisitive children. His plans, he said, were to spend most of his time aboard his "hobby," as he called her, cruising to England, Italy, Greece, Russia and perhaps even Spitzbergen and Iceland. Then he might sail down along the continent of South America. And as he dreamed of his far-ranging adventures, he hit upon the notion of naming his yacht after the legendary royal barge that had dazzled Mark Antony two thousand years earlier.

No doubt Cleopatra herself would have been impressed by the vessel; certainly George's Salem friends were. When *Cleopatra's Barge* was finally launched on October 21, 1816, they were invited to inspect her. They marveled at the sumptuous main cabin, as elegant as the finest Salem parlor, with paneled walls, a beamed ceiling, a fireplace and mahogany furniture. The Reverend William Bentley praised the yacht's graceful "settees with velvet cushions, chairs with descriptive paintings, mirrors, buffets loaded with plate of every name, and the best glass and porcelain." A sharp-eyed Salem lady noted other fine details: "The beams of the ceiling are edged with a gilt beading," she wrote to a friend, "and two ropes covered with red silk velvet twisted with gold cord are passed along, to take hold of when the vessel rolls. There are two elegant sofas, about the length of four chairs each, the seats of similar velvet; a border of gold lace on the edge and a deep red fringe. The design on the back is four harps, the strings of large brass wire, and the wood mahogany and burnt maple."

Becket's bill came to $50,000, three times what it cost in 1816 to build a fine merchantman of equivalent size. The length of the yacht was 100 feet overall and her beam nearly 23 feet; she drew 11½ feet and was rated at 192 tons. She was a hermaphrodite brig, with square sails on her foremast and fore-and-aft sails on her main. Her rakish lines, not to mention her 12 gunports, gave her the look of a warship rather than a cruising yacht. But there could be no mistaking her for a normal ship of any kind, for George had added two eccentric embellishments: a wooden Indian in full war paint on deck, and a different design on each side of her hull. From bow to stern along her starboard side were wide, vivid horizontal stripes of different colors; and on her port side was a dancing herringbone pattern. Evidently, for whimsical reasons he never bothered to explain, George intended her to look like two different ships to observers passing her on opposite sides.

His whimsy was matched by that of the man he designated as official clerk of the new yacht, Samuel Curwen Ward, who described the *Barge's* intended itinerary thusly: "To one or more ports, places, cities, islands, townes, boroughs, villages, bays, harbours, basins, rivers, creeks, lakes, inlets, outlets, situated in the known world, between the latitude of the Cape of Good Hope and the Arctic Circle." The sharp-eyed Salem woman who had taken such a quick inventory of the yacht's furnishings offered a guess at one of George's destinations: Around the walls of the main cabin, she reported, "is a row of gilt hat-pins, perhaps for the King

of Naples to hang his hat on, as I hear the captain says the royal guest is to sit on that sofa.'' George, as his friend divined, had ambitious plans that went beyond simple cruising. He hoped to use his floating palace as a place to entertain royalty, and he was aiming for even bigger game than King Ferdinand of Naples.

To the rest of the Crowninshield family, it all seemed a bit pretentious. Brother Ben, Secretary of the Navy, was embarrassed when told that the yacht had been christened *Cleopatra's Barge*, resignedly remarking to his wife, Mary, that he supposed it was inevitable that George would choose ''some foolish name that would be laughed at.'' Sister Sarah and brother John ridiculed the project so openly that George, who had included them in his will, changed it to leave them only $10 each. But he was too pleased with his new plaything to be angry with everybody. When an opportunistic cousin sent a barrel of mincemeat to the yacht—with a bill for $160—George muttered but paid for it. His sister-in-law Mary found George's pleasure infectious. In a letter to her husband in Washington, she commented that George ''appears so happy and satisfied with himself, much as our boys are with their new sled. I envy him his feelings.'' George had just dropped in on her, ''all powdered & dressed in his fur coat going to ride out to his brig in a sleigh today. This has not been done in this town in fifteen years.''

Indeed, it was an uncommonly cold winter even for Salem, with ice that was thick enough in the harbor not only to support horses but also to encase *Cleopatra's Barge* at her mooring. George used the time productively, however, adding to the yacht's rich furnishings: a magnificent tea urn, graceful cream pitchers, silver butter and fish knives, and an abundance of fine china. He ordered green-and-gold liveries for his steward and the ship's boys. The final touch was a golden cat, named Pompey, to lounge on the couches and on George's four-postered, canopied bed in the master stateroom.

George was of course qualified by his experience as a captain in the Crowninshield fleet to command his new vessel. But this was a luxury yacht, and its owner should not be bothered with the captain's duties. He asked his cousin Benjamin Crowninshield, a 58-year-old blue-water veteran, to take command. Ben in turn brought along his son Benjamin Jr., who was planning to go to school in Europe. The two were distinguished from each other with the nicknames of ''Captain Ben'' at the *Barge's* helm and his son ''Philosopher Ben,'' who was regarded as the family's intellectual. Philosopher Ben was also a snob who thoroughly disapproved of his ostentatious cousin and repaid George's hospitality by keeping a journal that dripped with scorn, though it did provide a lively account of the *Barge's* madcap voyage.

While the yacht lay locked in the ice, George completed mustering his crew: eight seamen, three ship's boys, steward Hanson Posey (a freed slave) and cook William Chapman (another black man, who claimed to have served with Captain James Cook in the South Pacific). The members of the crew were provided with an opportunity for a shakedown cruise—along with what seemed like half the population of Salem—during a brief January thaw. But then the ice formed once again, blocking the harbor all through the month of February. George passed the time entertaining the curiosity seekers who came in an endless procession. He proudly wrote to his brother in Washington that more than 900 visitors per day crowded aboard the yacht; in fact, he boasted, "I have had 1,900 women & 700 men in one day."

The Secretary of the Navy relented enough to arrange for his brother to receive letters of introduction to the United States consuls and the commanders of United States Navy vessels in Europe, as well as other persons who might be helpful. In the end, George wound up with nearly 300 letters. When at last the ice moved out of Salem harbor, with *Cleopatra's Barge* following it on March 30, 1817, George Jr.'s yacht was setting sail under the most auspicious circumstances.

Promptly, on her second day out, she ran into a northeaster. Snow swirled across her deck, and a waterspout came threateningly close. *Cleopatra's Barge* shouldered her way through the storm with impressive sturdiness and settled down on course at a fast clip—so fast that at first the crew members did not believe her log. She was racing along at eight knots in moderate breezes and up to 11 in freshening winds. George was ecstatic. "She proves everything I could wish," he wrote.

Except for the red cord suspended overhead to hold onto in a rough sea, the 19-by-20-foot dining saloon of Cleopatra's Barge, here reconstructed in Salem's Peabody Museum, might have been the parlor of a New England shipowner's mansion. Crowninshield shared the saloon during his 1817 cruise with sailing companions who included cousin "Captain Ben" (top inset), and the captain's son, a student nicknamed "Philosopher Ben" (bottom inset).

The yacht was not the only thing that provided a spectacular display; so did the Atlantic Ocean during one phosphorescent night. Samuel Ward, whom George had designated as the *Barge's* clerk, kept the log. His entries, occasionally inspired by over-indulgence in the ship's brandy, included more than the routine laconic comments on course and weather, especially after he had spent an evening watching the phosphorescence that was stirred up by *Cleopatra's Barge.* "She appeared to be moving on waves of fire," he wrote. "Upon looking over the stern a bright stream of light seemed to dart from her rudder, and extend itself to a great distance behind. On each of the quarters other streams proceeded parallel with that from the rudder. They gave light enough to read the name on our stern."

Ward went forward and found a similar play of phosphorescence: "There appeared nothing but rows of brilliant fire, sparkling and foaming under the bows, and moving off in right angles on both sides of the ship, and fading into the darkness of the surrounding sea." Two pilot whales, attracted by the light, surfaced and frolicked ahead of the yacht. While Ward watched them, the *Barge* pitched into a high wave; "a sea came over our bows and drenched me from head to foot. Upon looking down at our deck, I found it covered with brilliant stars, and my shoes were ornamented with several studs, that shone elegantly."

Quite a different journal of the cruise was being kept by Philosopher Ben Crowninshield. The captain's son considered himself an excellent navigator; he had studied under Salem's own Nathaniel Bowditch, a mathematical genius and the author of the most important navigational treatise of the day. So young Ben was understandably puzzled when his cousin George ordered all sails shortened to prepare for an impending gale; George had dreamed of wild horses the previous night, and he was sure they portended bad weather, despite a steady barometer. The barometer turned out to be correct. Ben was even more baffled when George called for all the yacht's hatches to be opened to ventilate the belowdecks area—and also, George claimed, to make the ship more buoyant and increase her speed. A few boarding seas, cascading down the hatches, caused the opposite effect.

Nor was Philosopher Ben philosophical about the yachting party's first contact with the culture of the Old World, which occurred in the Azores. It started promisingly enough: The United States consul in Fayal, evidently impressed by the Secretary of the Navy's letter—and no doubt by *Cleopatra's Barge*—honored the American visitors with a lavish ball. "Good humor and hilarity prevailed," Ben wrote. So convivial was the party that on their return to the yacht through Fayal's dark streets, Captain Ben fell off the sidewalk and Samuel Ward wrenched his knee in a gully.

When George invited some islanders to come aboard the following day, however, the wind piped up and the yacht began to roll at her anchorage. Before long, Ben recorded, "several of the ladies were seasick, and none of them could walk upright." The women were handed down into the tender; a rain squall swept across the harbor and drenched them. "The Portuguese gentlemen," Ben sniffed, "behaved most ungallantly," remaining on board the yacht, "charmed with our accommodations and fascinated with our wine." They did not go ashore until dark. Philosopher Ben found the Azorians singularly unattractive: "They smell as strong as pole cats."

The yachting party was welcomed at the *Barge's* next port, Madeira, by the Governor of the island, and the United States consul entertained the company at a "superb dinner," Ben wrote. George reciprocated with a reception on board the yacht that seems to have attracted most of the population of the island. "The space from our vessel to the shore," Ben reported, "was covered with boats, and alongside never less than fourteen, and sometimes more, fighting and running one another down to get alongside first."

The crew was put back to work as soon as the islands were left astern. George ordered the *Barge's* giltwork to be touched up and the yacht made shipshape while they sailed eastward. Then, as the voyagers approached the entrance to the Mediterranean, a cabin boy named Perkins fell overboard.

George was first into a lifeboat. But the tackle jammed; the boat swung wildly, and a seaman, jumping in to help, was thrown onto George's neck. The lines parted, the lifeboat capsized, and George and the seaman scrambled back up the yacht's side. The longboat was launched successfully, with George aboard. By this time the lifeboat had drifted half a mile astern. Perkins swam for it and was hanging on to its overturned keel when the longboat reached him. While George and the seamen picked up Perkins and righted and bailed out the lifeboat, Captain Ben brought the yacht about and ran down to pick them up. Another rescue was added to George's long list.

Cleopatra's Barge touched at Tangier, and then turned northeast for brief stops at Gibraltar, Malaga, Cartagena and Majorca, before a longer visit to Barcelona. There, the *Barge* was inundated with the largest throng of her entire cruise. It was, Philosopher Ben commented, as "if an archangel had lighted on this earth." During the next few days, more than 20,000 Spaniards swarmed up the yacht's sides, across her decks and through all her cabins. George hospitably welcomed everyone aboard, invited as many as possible to dinner and gave everyone the run of the ship. Ben found his cabin crowded from breakfast to midnight; there were "friars with thick hoods and fat bellies, generals, colonels, etc., etc., dressed for the occasion, priests in black robes, and hats of three feet in diameter, and ladies, aye of every sort, colour, and size, under heaven. Never was there such a group, never such a crowd, and smell, since the days of Noah's Ark." When the harbor waters were rough, the yacht's rails were lined with seasick guests. The commodious main cabin was filled with such a jostling crush of bodies that one pregnant woman went into labor and was rushed ashore just in time. After five days of this, George set sail for Marseilles.

Cleopatra's Barge stayed at Marseilles for 15 days. Visitors continued to stream aboard: One nearsighted man strode up to the wooden Indian, doffed his hat and introduced himself. Meanwhile, George directed more refurbishing to repair the ravages of the visitors. Ben was moaning by now; they had done nothing, he wrote, "but alter and re-alter, change the colour of this part, retouch another." He complained, "We begin at daylight and go to bed in the middle of the night." But his cousin's burst of renovation had a purpose. George was preparing for what he regarded as the climax of his tour.

On the island of St. Helena, 4,000 miles away in the South Atlantic, was the most famous royal figure in the world: Napoleon Bonaparte, in exile after his final defeat at Waterloo two years earlier. Some of George's neighbors in Salem always suspected that their eccentric friend had planned to rescue Napoleon from his exile on the island. George never admitted as much, and probably he realized that the British Navy guard at St. Helena rendered such a scheme folly even for so romantic an adventurer as he. What George did openly plan was to attempt to make contact with Napoleon's family, especially his wife, Empress Marie Louise, in Rome.

Evidently George was convinced that Marie Louise would wish to leave Rome and join her husband, and he intended to offer *Cleopatra's Barge* as the vehicle of the royal reunion. Putting into Leghorn, located on Italy's northwest coast, George traveled overland to Florence, and from there he sent a message—accompanied by several of his letters of introduction—to the Empress.

Marie Louise, it happened, was quite content in Rome, where she was living luxuriously—with a lover and most of the Bonaparte family—on the fortune amassed during Napoleon's 11 years as Emperor. The Empress was not in the least tempted to exchange opulent Rome for barren St. Helena. She ignored the written entreaties of George Crowninshield, who ruefully returned to his yacht.

Still undaunted, George sailed on to Elba, the site of Napoleon's first exile. The stubby Emperor had by now become an obsession with the tubby yachtsman. At Elba, George acquired a pair of boots that Napoleon had rejected as too tight (they were too tight for George, too), and letters of introduction to the Bonapartes from a colonel who had served with the Emperor. George then took his yacht to Civitavecchia, the coastal port of Rome, and took the post chaise up to the Eternal City. Nine days later he was back, gleefully reporting that he had been entertained by the Bonapartes and exhibiting more mementoes: a portrait of the Emperor presented to George by Napoleon's mother, and a lock of the great man's hair. No Bonapartes accompanied him, but he brought along an odd group of six Frenchmen, one of whom claimed to be Napoleon's adopted son. With the new guests aboard, *Cleopatra's Barge* set sail on August 18 for Corsica, where her owner evidently planned more Napoleonic research.

By this time he must have aroused suspicion, because four French men-of-war kept watch on the yacht as she left Civitavecchia. And two days later, as she approached Corsica, she was met by one of the warships. George took the hint. He headed for Gibraltar. The naval vessel followed the *Barge* for a few miles until the yacht was out of French waters, and then turned back.

By September 1, with the yacht anchored at Gibraltar, Napoleon's "adopted son" had been revealed as a fraud whom the Bonapartes had been only too glad to urge onto the impetuous American. He and the

A pair of Napoleon's boots was among the mementos collected by Crowninshield when he called at Elba, site of the Emperor's first exile. Crowninshield did not, however, try to visit the well-guarded island of St. Helena, where Napoleon was exiled after the Battle of Waterloo.

other Frenchmen were happy to have a free ride to America, and George could think of no way to get rid of them. Philosopher Ben, however, finally went ashore to pursue his studies in Europe. Summing up his assessment of George, Ben concluded, "He is the greatest lump of deception in the whole world of man."

Cleopatra's Barge hauled her anchor out of the Mediterranean mud for the last time on September 2, 1817, and set her course for home. She arrived in Salem harbor, to a rousing welcome, on October 3. The Frenchmen disembarked and the yacht's crew was paid off. But George remained aboard the vessel, supervising a complete refit. Already he was making plans for an even more ambitious cruise to England, the North Sea and the Baltic.

On the evening of November 26, he had dinner with a friend named John Dodge. As they talked after dinner, Dodge noticed that George seemed chilled and huddled close to the cabin's fireplace. Dodge went ashore. At about nine that evening, George called for his steward, Hanson Posey. "I feel dreadfully," he complained, and asked for a gin and water. Before Posey could fetch it, his master fell to the cabin floor, dead of a heart attack. He was 51 years old.

George's old friend, the Reverend William Bentley, kept the death watch in the master's stateroom of *Cleopatra's Barge* that night. "What an awful contrast," he recalled, "when I sat with a shimmering taper by the body of my friend in the place which once gave him so much pleasure and now had become his tomb!"

Cleopatra's Barge was sold at auction for less than a third of what it had cost to build her. She was stripped of her furnishings, which were distributed among the Crowninshield family. She went into the South American trade, her once-lavish belowdecks loaded with hides, sugar, tapioca and coffee. For a while she served as a packet between Boston and Charleston, South Carolina. Then, in 1820, she had a brief return to glory. She was taken around Cape Horn and sold, at more than her original cost, to King Kamehameha II of the Hawaiian Islands, who renamed her *Pride of Hawaii*. Again she was a luxury yacht, and at last entertaining royalty. On April 5, 1824, without the King aboard, the crew got drunk and ran *Cleopatra's Barge* onto a reef off Kauai. Salvage attempts failed, and she was left on the reef, where she broke up and slowly disintegrated in the Pacific surf.

George Crowninshield Jr. belonged to no yacht club because in 1816 there was no yacht club in his homeland. The Americans did not found a substantial yacht club until almost midcentury. The earliest attempt, a New York association called the Knickerbocker Boat Club, dissolved the same year it was formed, in 1811. A New York Boat Club, begun in 1830, was also short-lived. Had George Crowninshield lived into his seventies, he might have had an opportunity to join the Boston Boat Club, started by 18 yachtsmen in 1834; but this one, too, quickly folded, a victim of the business panic of 1837.

The oldest American yacht club to survive to modern times is the Detroit Boat Club, founded originally as a rowing club on the Detroit River in 1839. Not until 1844 did the Americans establish a yacht club to

New York's yachting sanctum

At its founding in 1844, the New York Yacht Club—destined to become the citadel of American yachting—was a mere harbor-front cottage. And for more than a half century after this humble nativity, until a clubhouse was constructed on a lot donated by J. P. Morgan, the members held their meetings in hotels or restaurants, or rented space in buildings around the city.

But temporary quarters did not dim the glitter of such club festivities as the 47th anniversary dinner pictured at right. The clubhouse at that time was a rented three-story brick building that had formerly been a dancing school; its ballroom provided an imposing repository for half models of nearly a hundred members' yachts, and its ceiling was high enough to accommodate most of the members' private ensigns. The members themselves were equally lofty, including such eminent names as Astor, Goelet, Roosevelt, Vanderbilt and Whitney.

In addition to prestige, the New York Yacht Club offered a number of practical advantages. The club maintained stations along Long Island and the New England shore, where members could pick up supplies and mail. For the many members who commuted by yacht between waterfront mansions and Manhattan offices, the club provided two private piers—one at the foot of 26th Street in the East River and the other at 35th Street in the Hudson.

One member put his yacht to a practical use that was singularly reprehensible. In direct violation of the law, William C. Corrie in 1858 transported a cargo of 300 slaves from West Africa to the United States in his schooner *Wanderer*. On learning of Corrie's deed—and hearing, to their further horror, that *Wanderer* had flown the club's burgee at the time—the members unanimously resolved that, because of "his being engaged in a traffic repugnant to humanity and to the moral sense of the members of the Association, be he hereby expelled from the New York Yacht Club." For years, members were forbidden to mention either *Wanderer*'s name or that of her disgraced owner.

In the flag-hung Model Room of their clubhouse, New York Yacht Club members gather at a formal dinner in 1891. Members' wives were invited to tea earlier the same day, but they were excluded from the banquet in the evening.

match the prestige of England's Royal Yacht Squadron, which by then was more than a quarter of a century old. Its United States counterpart was the New York Yacht Club, organized by nine yachtsmen aboard *Gimcrack*, the yacht belonging to the club's first commodore, John Cox Stevens, an inventor and ship-line owner.

Gimcrack, although a comfortable craft at 51 feet, could not be called a luxury yacht. Neither could any of the other American pleasure craft that were proliferating during the first half of the 19th Century. Most American yachtsmen at this stage were not especially interested in luxury. Unlike their European brethren, they were not habitual clubmen, nor did title and privilege of rank particularly appeal to them. While a majority of Britain's yachtsmen were gentlemen with inherited fortunes, most of the yachtsmen in America had made—and were still making—their own fortunes. Fifteen of the first 17 commodores of the New York Yacht Club, for example, earned salaries—enormous ones, to be sure. They were pragmatic and self-reliant men who had achieved their success in a world that was fiercely competitive. In consequence, the New York Yacht Club was founded primarily in order to encourage racing, usually for sizable wagers.

But the steam-propelled vessel, which was finally coming of age, would soon serve to give American yachting a luxurious dimension. Fittingly, the man who would show the way—and establish a standard of opulence every bit as high as that of George Crowninshield in his time—had amassed much of his fortune from steamers.

Cornelius Vanderbilt started his spectacular career at the age of 16, with $100 borrowed from his mother. From a single boat transporting produce and passengers between Manhattan and Staten Island in 1810, he expanded his operations (ruthlessly, as his competitors learned to their regret); within half a century he had a fleet of 66 vessels. Some were ferries, others were chartered to the Union Navy during the Civil War, and still others traded around the world. Like Crowninshield, Vanderbilt was vain and egocentric. A skipper of his own vessels during his younger days, he was pleased when the press started calling him "Commodore"; few would risk his disfavor by ignoring his grandiloquent title. Unlike Crowninshield, Vanderbilt earned every nickel of his fortune, which amounted to more than $11 million by 1853; he was the richest man in America.

Having worked so hard to acquire this fortune, the Commodore decided that it was time to enjoy some of it. What better way than aboard the most luxurious yacht ever built? And where would he take her? To Europe, of course, as Crowninshield had, to impress the Old World's royalty with the new-won magnificence of America. Cornelius Vanderbilt joined the New York Yacht Club and placed an order with Jeremiah Simonson's shipyard in Greenport, Long Island, for America's first steam yacht. *North Star*, as she was christened, was a paddle-wheeler, with two masts for auxiliary sails. She was a "monster steamer," as one visitor described her—270 feet long and 38 feet wide between her two 34-foot-diameter paddle wheels.

A monster she may have appeared from the outside, but her interior was as attractive as it was palatial. Vanderbilt and his wife, Sophia,

Plowing steadily upwind through the blustery Atlantic, one of America's first large steam yachts, the 270-foot North Star, owned by Cornelius Vanderbilt (inset), relies on her steam engines and her 34-foot-wide paddle wheels. She used her sails mainly to steady her in the seas.

had 12 children. There was ample room aboard *North Star* to accommodate all of them in the style to which the Vanderbilts had become accustomed. Two of the children elected to stay home. The other 10, along with six sons-in-law, one daughter-in-law and a granddaughter, boarded the steam yacht in May of 1853. The family spread out into *North Star's* 10 private staterooms and settled down to enjoy their floating palace. The yacht's main saloon was furnished with Louis XV rosewood chairs and sofas, padded with velvet cushions. Another huge cabin, the reception saloon, held a sprawling sofa that seated 20 people. But the showpiece of the yacht was the dining room, a veritable banquet hall paneled in marble and granite, with a ceiling decorated by medallion portraits of such New World heroes as Christopher Columbus, George Washington and Daniel Webster.

North Star also contained a number of smaller staterooms, which for

An Arctic adventure that went awry

Newspaper publisher James Gordon Bennett Jr. knew how to use his yachts for business as well as for pleasure, and especially for promoting himself and his Paris and New York *Heralds*. His most dramatic maritime stunt was to bankroll a probe of the Arctic by the yacht *Jeannette*.

Bennett purchased the steam yacht in 1877 and promptly donated her—along with funds for a crew of 33—to the United States Navy as an exploration vessel. After voyaging around the Horn to San Francisco, *Jeannette* set sail for the edge of the Arctic ice pack on July 8, 1879; from there the exploration party was to go overland to the Pole. The *New York Herald* periodically reported sightings of the yacht as she made her way through Bering Strait. In early September she was seen near an island north of Siberia. Thereafter, nothing was heard of her for more than two years.

As it turned out, *Jeannette* became locked in Siberian ice just four days after the last sighting, and she remained embedded for 21 months. On June 13, 1881, she sank after cracking apart, and the crew set out over the ice pack for the mainland some 600 miles away. Eight men drowned en route and 12 died of exposure before the refugees could make their way home, not by ship but overland through Russia. The *Herald*, more dutifully than pridefully, reported the disaster. But Bennett himself remained uncharacteristically silent, even during a subsequent Navy inquiry.

As caricatured by the magazine Vanity Fair, a dapper James Gordon Bennett Jr. reposes on a trunk labeled with the ports of call of his oceangoing yachts.

With Jeannette encased in the ice, her crew members explore the surrounding floes. To augment their supplies, they hunted polar bears, seals and walrus.

OFF TO THE POLE

Departure of the Steamer Jeannette from San Francisco

CALIFORNIA'S HEARTY "GOODBY."

Ten Thousand People Cheer the Gallant Explorers.

THROUGH THE GOLDEN GATE.

Sketches of the Officers and Men of the American Expedition.

[BY TELEGRAPH TO THE HERALD.]

SAN FRANCISCO, July 8, 1879.

several days past the weat

Bennett publicized Jeannette's departure in huge headlines, claiming that 10,000 San Franciscans swarmed to watch her departure for the Arctic.

her maiden voyage were occupied by the family physician and a chaplain and their wives. Vanderbilt's captain was a clipper-ship veteran, Asa Eldridge (who also brought his wife). Many of the members of the crew were volunteers from New York's wealthy families, eager to take part in the adventure. Deep in *North Star's* hull was a gang of professional coal stokers. Their reaction to the yacht's magnificence was not much to Vanderbilt's liking, however; an hour before time for departure they struck for higher wages.

Vanderbilt fired all of them on the spot, and instructed Captain Eldridge to comb the waterfront for anyone who could wield a shovel. Eldridge succeeded in recruiting a new engine-room crew, and on May 19, *North Star* dropped her lines from her East River pier. Her paddle wheels churned and she went thunking into the harbor, where she promptly ran aground.

A passing steamer helped haul her off, and the yacht was towed to a navy yard for repairs. Soon she was moving grandly down New York Harbor again, then out into the Atlantic, bound for England. Day after day, with or without wind, she moved steadily northeastward, averaging 13 knots and burning 42 tons of coal every 24 hours. The chaplain, John Choules, kept a journal, obsequiously praising Vanderbilt's "fine tact" and "dignified self-control." An incident Choules omitted, however, occurred one evening when Vanderbilt offered his son William $10,000 if he would quit smoking. "Oh, father," his son replied, "you don't have to bribe me. Your wish is enough." The Commodore responded by blowing a mouthful of cigar smoke into his son's face.

For 11 days *North Star's* passengers promenaded the yacht's spacious decks, dined grandly and gathered after dinner in the main saloon while the ladies serenaded them and the chaplain led them in prayers, to the accompaniment of the rhythmic swish of the tireless paddle wheels. On June 1, *North Star* passed between the shores of England's south coast and the cliffs of the Isle of Wight—and ran aground in the Solent.

A rising tide freed her, however, and she swept into Southampton to be greeted by cheering crowds. Like Crowninshield, Vanderbilt welcomed the thousands who swarmed aboard to marvel at the yacht. The city fathers entertained him at a banquet, and the Commodore responded by inviting 400 officials and merchants aboard the yacht for a sail around the Isle of Wight. The excursion ended with Vanderbilts and guests waltzing on *North Star's* deck, and the departing Britons raising three cheers for their host.

But, again like Crowninshield, Vanderbilt failed to attract any of Britain's royalty aboard his yacht. Some of the press compared him to the Medicis; the royal family, however, evidently was sensitive to the point that one newspaper voiced politely but patronizingly: Praising the Commodore as a self-made man, the editor suggested that "it is time that *parvenu* should be looked on as a word of honor."

Vanderbilt's ego was finally assuaged when, after a short call at Copenhagen, *North Star* put into Kronstadt, Russia. The Grand Duke Constantine, High Admiral of the Russian Navy, came aboard, accompanied by numerous admirals. To the Commodore's delight, the Grand Duke was so impressed by the yacht that he asked permission to have some of

his officers study and sketch her. While Russian engineers and artists swarmed through the vessel, Vanderbilt visited The Hermitage in St. Petersburg. *North Star* had scarcely set out again across the Baltic when Czar Alexander ordered a steam yacht of his own.

For Vanderbilt the remainder of *North Star's* cruise was something of an anticlimax, marred also by tragedy: In the Bay of Biscay, en route to the Mediterranean, a quartermaster named Robert Flint, one of the well-bred young volunteers, fell overboard and drowned. Two weeks later, off Leghorn, the voyagers were forcibly reminded of Italy's war of unification when gunboats suddenly came out to surround the yacht. It developed that the local authorities had become alarmed at the sight of the large vessel looming offshore, and suspected *North Star* of ferrying revolutionaries to attack Italy's Austrian rulers. "Austrian imagination," wrote Choules, "could not conceive of such a ship being the ocean home of a private American merchant."

By this time the American merchant was getting restless. It did not help matters when *North Star's* papers turned out not to include sufficient documentation to satisfy the suspicious port officers at Civitavecchia and Naples, with the result that no one was allowed to go ashore. Vanderbilt went on to Malta, but did not stay there long enough even to accept the British Governor's invitation to a reception. The summer was waning. Vanderbilt had been away from his office for more than three months. After making a quick stop at Constantinople, *North Star* turned toward the west.

Gibraltar, Tangier and Madeira were touched only briefly on the way home. And on September 23, 1853, *North Star* raced into New York Harbor without even waiting to pick up a pilot. Back in the business world, Vanderbilt quickly saw that two of his partners had double-crossed him during his absence by forming their own shipping line to Nicaragua. He declared his intentions in a terse note: "Gentlemen: You have undertaken to cheat me. I won't sue you, for the law is too slow. I'll ruin you. C.V."

Vanderbilt dissolved the partnership. Deciding that he had had enough yachting, he cannily sold *North Star* to the new line. Then, using his influence with the Central American governments, he strangled his former partners' line and put them out of business.

Vanderbilt plunged back into his own multifaceted business for the rest of his life and never went cruising again. When he died in 1877, he was worth more than $100 million.

Cornelius Vanderbilt had done his part to popularize the steam yacht. And the Civil War speeded up the development of the steam vessel. In fact, when the members of the New York Yacht Club voted at the outbreak of the War to volunteer their sailing yachts for naval service, only two were accepted—an indication of the increasing importance of steam. By 1870 the New York Yacht Club had four steam yachts in its fleet; by 1880 the number had risen to 20; by 1890 there were 71.

One of the most ardent proponents of steam was James Gordon Bennett Jr. It was no easy task to outdo Cornelius Vanderbilt in seagoing luxury, but Bennett succeeded.

A silver trophy donated to the New York Yacht Club by James Gordon Bennett Jr. is adorned with steam yachts and mermaids. Although the club sponsored a few races for steam yachts, contests for sailing yachts remained the chief sporting fare.

On the foredeck of James Gordon Bennett Jr.'s Namouna,
awnings protect the passengers from the Adriatic sun while the
yacht cruises off Venice in 1890. Bennett, in three-piece
suit and straw boater (left), talks to one of his many lady guests.

Bennett's father was an austere Scot who had made his fortune in a most unlikely way: He published a scandal-mongering newspaper, the *New York Herald*. He was a pariah to New York's social elite and once said that "American society consists of the people who don't invite me to their parties." His son was more acceptable. Handsome, bright, rich and daring, he exuded charm. He became a member of the New York Yacht Club at 16, and in the course of his colorful yachting career he would be twice elected commodore.

He started in schooners. His *Henrietta*—a swift vessel rated at 158 tons—was one of the two sailing yachts accepted by the Union Navy. Young Bennett himself was commissioned a lieutenant in the revenue cutter service (in return, it was said, for his father's support for the Union cause in the editorial pages of the *Herald*). The new lieutenant offered so much unsolicited advice to his superior officers, however, that his resignation was accepted after a few months. His doting father gave him a job at the *Herald*, a large allowance and, a year after the end of the War, the paper itself.

Bennett Jr. proved to be as dynamic a newspaper publisher as his father was, making the *Herald*—and, not incidentally, himself—world-famous for such exploits as sending journalist Henry M. Stanley into Africa to find missionary David Livingstone (who did not consider himself lost). In 1882 he built the 227-foot *Namouna* for $200,000. Her massive boilers, supplemented by the sails on her three masts, could speed her at 14 knots on the frequent transatlantic runs between Bennett's offices in New York and those of another *Herald* that he established in Paris. *Namouna* was an English mansion afloat, with cabins and staterooms paneled in oak, maple, cherry, chestnut and teak. Bennett's huge cherrywood bed alone cost $1,000. The yacht's staterooms were positioned toward the bow—a reversal of sailing-yacht practice but a sensible arrangement in a steamer, since the funnels often coated the after-deck with soot. Some of the bathrooms showed still further design innovation: a tub sunk beneath a trap door, providing more floor area. The yacht was jammed with expensive clutter, like every Victorian parlor; in *Namouna's* case, there were Oriental rugs, plush furniture and an elaborate mantelpiece in the main saloon hung with figurines, plates, a sword and—evidently Bennett's evocative contribution—a human skull of unknown origin.

Fifty officers and men staffed *Namouna*. Upkeep and the salaries of the crew cost Bennett $48,000 a year and, with *Namouna's* appetite for coal, helped run her annual overall expense up to $150,000. But Bennett made extensive use of the yacht—to the rue of some of his associates. Members of the *Herald's* staff, who were frequently summoned aboard, gave *Namouna* the nickname *Pneumonia*, unaccustomed as they evidently were to life at sea. Bennett could be mischievously eccentric. He particularly hated playing cards. At his orders, the crew's and his visitors' baggage was gone through for such contraband. His retaliation when he discovered a pack of cards was ingenious: He tore up the four aces and then returned the pack to the unsuspecting victim's luggage.

Considering Bennett's predilection for entertaining female guests aboard his yachts, it seems odd that he named his next one after Lysis-

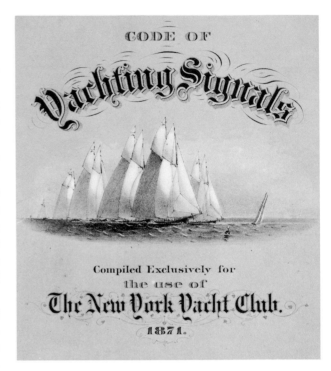

An attractive and useful aid to navigation for members of the New York Yacht Club, this code book was first issued in 1871. Confined to international signals used by yachtsmen, it replaced the bulkier commercial code book used by merchant captains. The club's book also listed recommended rules for such events as dinners and balls aboard yachts.

trata, the ancient Greek heroine who—as recounted by the playwright Aristophanes—led a boycott of marital relations that persuaded Athens' fighting men to end the Second Peloponnesian War. Bennett's *Lysistrata* was a proud beauty. The ultimate for her time, she was unmatched for personal appointments by anything in the United States or Europe. She was designed and built abroad—conceived by Britain's preeminent yacht architect, George Watson, and constructed in Dumbarton, Scotland, in 1900. She was 314 feet long and cost more than $600,000, a nearly unheard-of sum even in the splendid age of palatial steam yachts. *Lysistrata* had huge reception rooms and cabins for dozens of guests. There were so many staterooms that Bennett could reserve for himself a suite on each of the three decks. Among *Lysistrata*'s amenities were a Turkish bath and a padded cabin for an Alderney cow, which was kept content by an electric fan; she provided fresh milk for Bennett and his guests with the aid of an electric milking machine. The guests included Bennett's many mistresses ("There were curious tales concerning his fancies," recalled Consuelo Vanderbilt, the Commodore's great-granddaughter). All this floating hospitality required a crew of 100.

As master of *Lysistrata*, Bennett proved more eccentric than ever. When an acting troupe came aboard during a visit to Amsterdam, Bennett found their performance so pleasing that he sailed off with them and would not put them ashore until they had completed their entire repertoire. Then there was his paranoia concerning beards. Convinced that the Royal Navy's preeminence on the sea could be credited to its clean-shaven officers and crewmen, Bennett would allow no bearded man on his yacht. One stubborn *Herald* staffer, James Creelman, refused to shave when he was summoned from Paris to meet Bennett for a conference aboard *Lysistrata* in Leghorn. Creelman was not permitted aboard. When *Lysistrata* sailed, Creelman followed her from port to port. Bennett refused to relent, and finally Creelman gave up and returned to Paris. Eventually he quit the *Herald* and joined a competing paper.

Another *Herald* employee, an editor, was given a uniquely demeaning assignment. He happened to be aboard *Lysistrata* one day in a French port when it became necessary to replace the yacht's cow (history does not record what happened to it). Bennett grabbed the editor and drove off across the French countryside in search of another prime specimen of Alderney. At last one was found; Bennett bought it, instructed the editor to walk it to the yacht, and drove off. Understandably, Bennett was unpopular with most of his employees. One of them, correspondent George W. Hosmer, no doubt summed up their feelings in his assessment of Bennett: "When sober he displayed the worst qualities of the Scotch and when drunk the worst qualities of the Irish."

In the end, *Lysistrata* helped bring him down. Beguiled by his life of floating luxury, Bennett devoted less and less time to the *Herald*. The newspaper's fortunes faded as his profligacies increased. When he died in 1918, at the age of 77, he was nearly broke, having squandered an estimated $40 million. Yachting had been a means of self-gratification as epic in scale as the energies of the land that produced him. Despite Hosmer's assessment of his Scottish or Irish qualities, Bennett's willfulness was unmistakably American.

"The finest pleasure craft"

Her designer, British marine architect George L. Watson, said she was his masterpiece, and a yachting reporter called her "the finest pleasure yacht afloat." Certainly *Margarita*, at 323 feet and 1,830 tons, was a miracle of yachtbuilding in 1900, when she was built at a cost of £100,000 for an American, Anthony J. Drexel, a banking partner of J. P. Morgan. Her 5,000-horsepower engine matched that of the 5,000-ton ocean liner *Britannic*. A double hull and 10 watertight compartments made her as safe as any ship afloat.

Margarita's amenities were no less impressive. She was heated by steam and cooled by a forced-draft ventilation system. Her electric plant lighted 800 bulbs throughout the yacht and powered a machine that made 1,200 pounds of ice daily. The appointments included balustraded staircases, paneled saloons, exquisite moldings and a veritable treasury of antiques. Operation of this seagoing pleasure palace required the attention of a 93-man crew.

Drexel used *Margarita* for only 11 years before selling her to Britain's Marquess of Anglesey. He renamed her *Semiramis*, cruised Europe in her, and in World War I turned her over to the Royal Navy. Later she was put up for charter but proved too expensive to operate. The end came in 1947; she was stripped of her splendor and broken up for scrap.

Margarita's clipper bow, slightly raked masts, and raised forecastle and quarterdeck gave her a classic profile. Her hull, originally white, was painted black by the Marquess of Anglesey.

The yacht's elaborately carved balusters and curved staircase were more appropriate to a palace than to a boat. The animal carving atop the baluster (right) was probably added by the Marquess of Anglesey, since it resembles his family crest.

Margarita's dining saloon featured a fireplace (inset) and rich paneling, and was furnished with ornate Chippendale antiques, including a ceiling-high buffet. Most of the china and bric-a-brac were stowed in wooden cases before the yacht left the harbor.

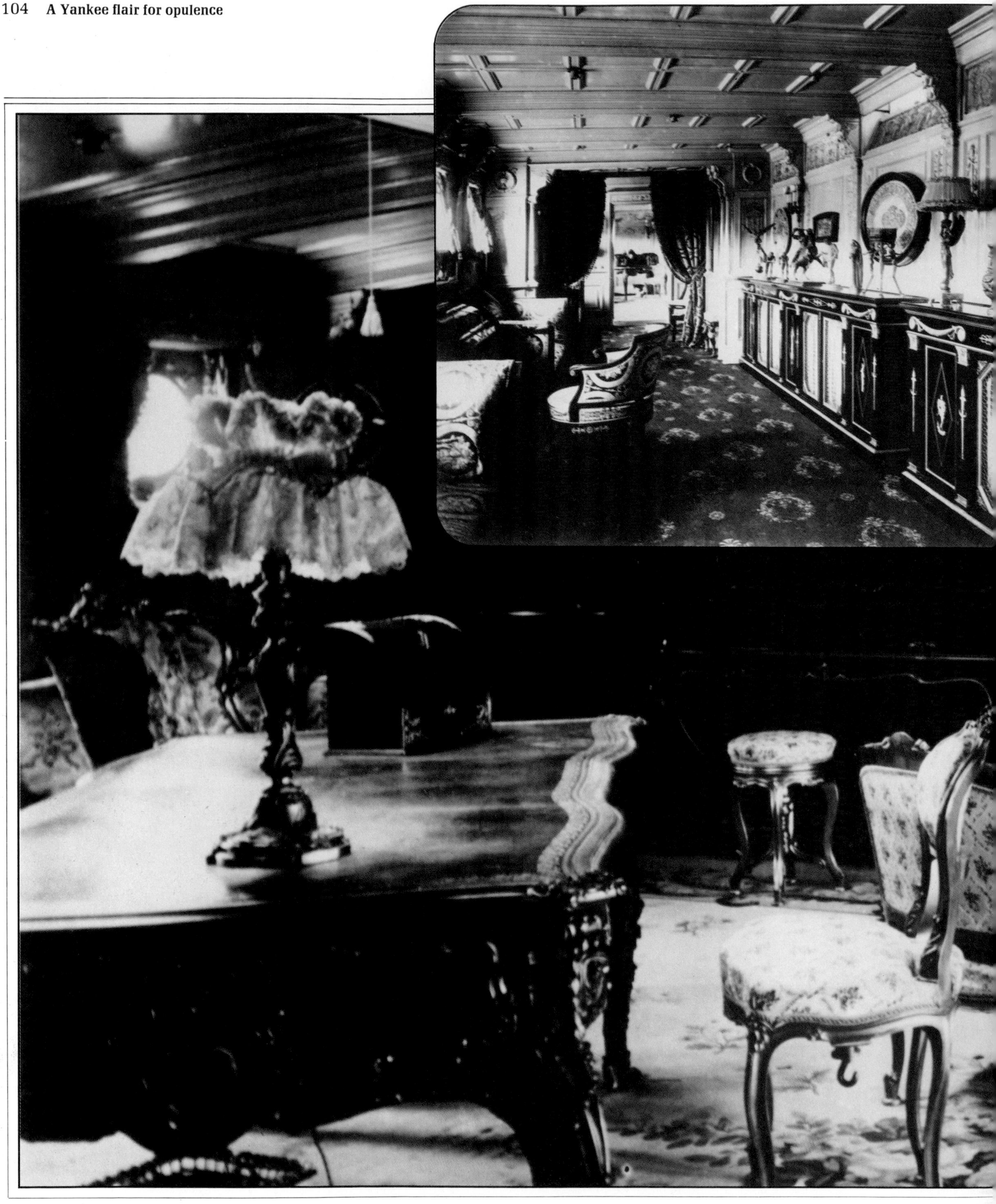

The Empire-style furnishings that graced Margarita's library (inset) complemented the Louis XV decor of the drawing room (below). Both rooms were distinguished by intricate paneling and coffered ceilings. The huge drawing room, with its rich carpeting, graceful sofas and massive desk, was one of the most splendid living spaces aboard any ship.

Chapter 4

Idylls of millionaires and kings

The international glamor of yachting is caught in a painting of guests aboard Cornelius Vanderbilt III's North Star at Cowes in 1909.

ow much does it cost to run a yacht?" asked millionaire oilman Henry Clay Pierce.

"You cannot afford to run a yacht," replied financier John Pierpont Morgan.

"Why? I'm pretty warm, you know."

"You have no right to own a yacht if you have to ask that question."

This bit of repartee has been repeated so often in one version or another that it has become yachting's most famous cliché. In fact, the exchange is probably apocryphal: There is no hard evidence that it ever occurred. It nevertheless epitomizes the period at the turn of the century when some American fortunes were so vast that the cost of pleasure was almost an irrelevancy.

The latter part of the 19th Century and the early years of the 20th saw unprecedented industrial growth in the United States, with railroads and electric lines crisscrossing the continent, and meat-packing plants, steel mills and oil refineries springing up to fill an ever-expanding demand. Since there were few laws to restrict cutthroat methods of business and virtually no income taxes, those who controlled the new industries amassed prodigious wealth. These new captains of industry built mansions on New York's Fifth Avenue and Italianate villas on Long Island and at Newport. They spent their new-won riches on paintings, antiques, rare *objets d'art*, thoroughbred horses—and, most spectacularly of all, on yachts. Theirs was a nobility of money, with a class structure as rigid as that of the blooded aristocrats of Europe.

To the titans of this Gilded Age, yachts were more than proof of position and instruments of leisure: A yacht often served business purposes as well. Commuting was one: Private steamers traveled incessantly between private docks on the Hudson River or Long Island Sound and private docks in Manhattan that were reserved by the New York Yacht Club for its members. Moreover, confidential negotiations could safely be held in the privacy of a yacht. In 1885, for example, J. P. Morgan used his steam yacht *Corsair* to help settle a potentially costly territorial dispute between the New York Central and the Pennsylvania Railroads. After inviting the officers of both railroads aboard *Corsair*, he refused to let them go ashore, steaming up and down the Hudson for a full day until they finally agreed to divide the territory, thus protecting Morgan's investment in the New York Central.

A Morgan yacht even played a military role. When the Spanish-American War erupted in 1898, the Navy requisitioned 21 New York Yacht Club steamers, including Morgan's second *Corsair*, a larger copy of the first, which he had sold. At first Morgan was annoyed: He had just been elected commodore of the club and was now without a flagship. But when *Corsair*, rechristened the U.S.S. *Gloucester*, sank one Spanish torpedo boat and disabled another at the Battle of Santiago, his pique turned to pride. Nonetheless, a yachtless existence did not suit him. Rather than await the second *Corsair*'s decommissioning, he instructed her designer to start on a third. She was launched in 1899. At 304 feet, she was larger than the first two but was a faithful copy down to the last detail (the carpets had to be custom milled, since the 1890 pattern had been discontinued).

J. P. Morgan (inset) owned three magnificent yachts in succession, all named Corsair. Here the second Corsair rides at anchor in Philadelphia in 1892. By this time, steam yachts like her carried only vestigial masts, which were used mainly to "dress ship" by flying rows of multicolored signal flags.

All around Morgan, yachtsmen young and old displayed an equal flair
for spending. George Lauder Jr., heir to a steel fortune, kept his 137-foot
schooner *Endymion* in New Haven harbor while he was a student at
Yale; it conveyed him home to Greenwich on weekends. *Endymion* was
manned by a crew of more than 20, most of them veteran Swedish sailors. On one occasion, a passing yachtsman, attracted by the tall masts in
New Haven harbor, went alongside and asked a deckhand if the owner
was aboard; the yachtsman felt obliged to record the man's reply: "No,
dey have him in yale. If he be good he be out Friday."

Young Lauder was generous with his toy. He once sent the yacht all
the way to Maine to pick up a friend whom he had invited to a party.
Another Yale yachtsman, railroad heir John Jay Phelps, was even more
openhanded. He invited a group of classmates aboard his 112-foot yacht
Brünhilde in 1885 for a postgraduate cruise. They circumnavigated the
world, returning home nearly three years later.

Predictably, the pacesetter in yachting expenditure was a Vanderbilt—William Kissam Vanderbilt, grandson of the "Commodore." In
1886 he presided over the launching of *Alva*. Named for his wife, *Alva*
was 285 feet long, cost half a million dollars and was the largest and most
expensive yacht that had yet been built in the United States. From her
clipper bow to her soaring stern, she was a graceful beauty. Three tall
masts carried her schooner rig, and two steam boilers in her hull supplemented her sails. The color scheme of her dining saloon—white enamel
ornamented in gold—set the formal tone for *Alva's* interior. Each of her
staterooms was done in a different wood; her library, 18 feet long and 16
feet wide, was paneled in French walnut.

Alva's launching was a major news event. A private train brought the
owner and his guests down from New York to the shipyard at Wilming-
ton, Delaware. Ten thousand people crowded the shoreline to watch the
big yacht slide down the ways. Vanderbilt and his family shortly set out
on a cruise to the West Indies, followed by a transatlantic voyage to
parade the yacht before European royalty. It is estimated that *Alva* cost
$5,000 a month to operate; Vanderbilt, of course, never had to ask how
much. In 1892 *Alva* collided with a freighter off Cape Cod and sank.
Vanderbilt immediately ordered a larger yacht.

Among the new-rich there was a considerable spirit of competition to
outdazzle one another. Jacob Lorillard exhibited his tobacco fortune by
purchasing a new yacht every year. Anthony J. Drexel, a Philadelphia
banker, bragged that few men in the world could afford the maintenance
he paid on his 323-foot steamer *Margarita:* She required a crew of 93 and
resembled a Newport mansion afloat. His next yacht, *Sayonara,* was
only 186 feet long but featured a formal garden on her deck, complete
with trellises and climbing roses. When the salt-laden winds killed the
roses Drexel had them replaced with artificial flowers made of rubber,
whose colors ran and stained the deck.

But the most conspicuous form of competition among the turn-of-the-
century United States yacht owners was speed. Wall Streeter George
Osgood boasted to fellow yachtsmen one day in 1881 that he had had
breakfast in his Newport home at 7 a.m. and had arrived in New York in
time for dinner nine hours later; his 185-foot steam yacht *Stranger* had

A rejected yachtsman's revenge

JAY GOULD

He issued fraudulent stock and shamelessly milked the companies he seized. Among the victims of his free-wheeling financial swindles were many members of the New York Yacht Club. So Jay Gould was doubtless more angered than surprised when, upon applying for membership in the prestigious club in the 1870s, he was blackballed.

In 1881, after skimming the cream from yet another of his dubious financial coups, Gould decided to devote more of his leisure time to yachting. He ordered the most advanced yacht in America—the fast, propeller-driven, 248-foot *Atalanta*—and outfitted her with expensive tapestries, a dining saloon that seated 32, electric lighting and a machine that could make half a ton of ice.

But Gould made no further effort to become a member of the New York Yacht Club. Instead, in 1883 he gathered a group of financiers and political bosses and put together his own organization, the American Yacht Club, located across the street from the one that had rejected him.

run down Long Island Sound at an average speed of 15 knots. To his peers, this had the distinct ring of challenge, but two years passed before *Stranger's* record was eclipsed by Jay Gould's 248-foot *Atalanta,* which could reach a top speed of 17 knots.

Many an owner was overcome with anguish as another yacht swept past him down Long Island Sound. When cotton millionaire Matthew C. D. Borden endured this humiliation he told his captain, "Don't stop at the yacht club landing. Continue on to Seabury's Yard so that I can order a faster yacht." One yachting writer pointed out that every American yachtsman "who gives an order for a steam yacht directs the builder to make it a little faster than any previous vessel, and thus the ingenuity of the enterprising builders is taxed to the uttermost, and excellence is the natural result."

Even if speed was the first consideration, a yacht's appointments were always an important yardstick of status. In this respect, no turn-of-the-century American yacht outshone a rakish beauty owned by yet another Vanderbilt, Cornelius III—the old Commodore's great-grandson and a nephew of William Kissam Vanderbilt. He not only bore the name of the family's founder but also owned a yacht named *North Star.* Although her length—256 feet—was about the same as that of the original *North Star,* she was far more lavish. Her cabins were filled with antiques, and elaborately paneled ceilings and walls were everywhere. The deep-carpeted dining saloon featured a wide fireplace with a marble mantel; so did the library. Some staterooms were nearly as large as the reception rooms. This second *North Star,* with her carved, clipper bow, had the long, lean hull that was to become the hallmark of the American luxury steam yacht. She had one smokestack and two vestigal masts that were used only for signaling.

Such a showplace afloat was the perfect setting for Cornelius Vanderbilt's wife, Grace. She came from a wealthy family herself (her father had made a fortune in cotton and in Southern railroads), and the lavishness of *North Star* was exceeded only by that of Beaulieu, her shoreside mansion in Newport. Grace Vanderbilt was—or considered herself to be—a pillar of United States society. And like most of the wealthy American society leaders, she looked to Europe as the example. She insisted on taking *North Star* to Cowes every summer so that she could see, and be seen by, the King and Queen. Her detractors called her "The Kingfisher," and her husband finally got so fed up that he bought another yacht—*Winchester,* more a destroyer than a yacht—retired aboard and left Beaulieu to his wife.

Most British yachtsmen continued to regard Americans as amusing parvenus, but there was at least one notable exception, an Irish-born magnate named Sir Thomas Lipton. He was a self-made man in the best American tradition. Indeed, he had traveled to the United States as a young man and had worked as a plantation hand, as a peddler and finally as a grocery clerk in New York City. Returning to the mother country at the age of 19, he parlayed a grocery business into a tea empire and became a friend and confidant of British royalty. Yet he never put on airs. "Fancy me, Tommy Lipton," he would chortle, his goatee bobbing, "going downstairs to dinner with a princess on each arm!" If Tommy Lipton could hobnob with British royalty, his American friends must have said to themselves, so could any millionaire—as long as he owned a proper yacht.

Lipton's own steam yacht had originally been built in Scotland for an Italian aristocrat and had been named *Aegusa*. When Sir Thomas bought her in 1898, he promptly renamed her *Erin*. (Ever the Irishman, he would challenge for the America's Cup with five racing yachts named *Shamrock*, over a period of three decades.) In outward appearance the 287-foot, 1,242-ton *Erin* was a classic of her day, with a clipper bow, a teak deckhouse, a large expanse of awninged deck, and a sharply raked transom dominated by a long, slender ensign staff. Her tall, yellow funnel was complemented by two raked masts, used only to fly steadying storm sails in rough weather and bunting during ceremonies.

Belowdecks, *Erin* was something special even to the aristocrats and millionaires who were invited aboard whenever she put into port. She gleamed with brass and polished wood. There was a harp in the music room, and the bulkheads were hung with watercolors. Each night at nine, guests dined formally under soft light glowing through blue lampshades; on an ordinary afternoon, some 70 people lunched on deck. Lipton's well-publicized entertaining aboard *Erin*, as much as his cheerful sportsmanship when all five of his America's Cup challengers failed, endeared him to millions of Americans, who gratifyingly gulped down billions of cups of Lipton's Tea. And American yachtsmen found Sir Thomas a strengthening bond between them and their counterparts across the Atlantic.

Another straightforward and spirited Briton who appealed to the Americans was Lady Anna Brassey, author of a yachting book that won a wide audience in the United States as well as in England. Her husband, Sir Thomas Brassey, was heir to a railroad fortune, a Member of Parliament and an expert yachtsman. Lady Brassey was quite at home presiding over banquets aboard Sir Thomas' steam-auxiliary schooner *Sunbeam*, but she was happier on the high seas. She told of one memorable cruise in a volume titled *Around the World in the Yacht Sunbeam*.

The yacht left Chatham on July 1, 1876. Aboard were the four Brassey children, five guests (including two officers of the Royal Navy), and a sizable crew: 18 sailors, two engineers, two firemen, four stewards and two cooks, not to mention a nurse, a stewardess and a maid. Also aboard at the start were two dogs, three birds, and a "charming Persian kitten belonging to the baby"; the Brasseys loved animals, as well as the sea.

Within a couple of days the kitten had slipped overboard; but it was replaced at another port by a cat named Lily. Even for a cat, keeping one's footing on *Sunbeam*'s deck was not easy. Heavily loaded with 84 tons of coal, 30 tons of extra equipment and a library of 700 books, she rode low in the water and was often swept in heavy weather, so her decks were usually wet. Daughter Mabelle Brassey was almost washed overboard during the first gale; she was saved at the last moment by a guest, Captain Squire Lecky of the Royal Navy, who grabbed her with one hand and a line from the boom with the other. "Hold on, Captain Lecky," Mabelle said calmly, "hold on." Lecky held on.

Secret theater for surgery

Ingenious use was made of a yacht in 1893 when banker E. C. Benedict's 138-foot *Oneida (below)* became an operating theater for a highly important patient. In June of that year, President Grover Cleveland's doctors diagnosed a malignant growth in his jaw. At the time, the country was in the middle of a financial crisis, and White House advisers feared it might develop into a full-blown business panic if the public learned the President's life was in danger.

Casting about for a clandestine way to treat the malady, they remembered that Cleveland had frequently been seen relaxing aboard his friend Benedict's yacht. Her main saloon was secretly outfitted for surgery, and a team of doctors slipped aboard. When Cleveland boarded *Oneida* in New York on Friday evening, June 30, everyone who saw him assumed that he was weekending with Benedict again.

The growth was removed the next morning, and *Oneida* continued her cruise while Cleveland recuperated. He came ashore five days later, publicly complaining of "a toothache." No hint of the secret operation leaked out for two months—and by that time Cleveland was well along the road to full recovery.

Two years after his operation aboard Oneida (below), President Cleveland used her to meet with J. P. Morgan to arrange a loan to the hard-pressed U.S. Treasury.

PRESIDENT GROVER CLEVELAND

Daughter Muriel was saved by another Royal Navy guest, Commander James Brown, who lifted her above the waters that were raging across the deck. "I'm not at all wet, I'm not!" Muriel shouted excitedly when she was put down. She was the only one on deck who had not been drenched by the boarding sea. "Happily, the children don't know what fear is," their mother wrote.

Sir Thomas took *Sunbeam* through the Strait of Magellan to avoid the blustery ocean off Cape Horn, and Anna Brassey was thrilled to watch spear-carrying "savages," as she called them, studying the yacht from the shores of Tierra del Fuego. In the Pacific and Indian Oceans, the equatorial heat turned the cabins into ovens and blistered the deck; it was so hot, Anna Brassey reported, that Sir Thomas even removed his jacket, waistcoat and stiff collar.

A Christmas display of an erupting volcano in the Hawaiian Islands— a "cloud of fire over Kilauea," she wrote—was followed by a tempestuous passage through the North Pacific to Japan. "Many of the sailors and servants were ill," Lady Brassey recorded. "I was hopelessly so." The children came down with influenza; the baby developed pleurisy and almost died. As they were approaching Japan, *Sunbeam* ran before a gale through a series of rocky islands, "among which the sea boiled, and seethed, and swirled," Anna wrote. Meanwhile the family, bundled in furs, watched from the wind-swept deck as another volcano lighted the stormy night sky.

From Japan, *Sunbeam* proceeded down the coast of China, across the Indian Ocean and through the Suez Canal. En route, the voyagers experienced all manner of adventures, including a fire that spread almost out of control when woodwork was ignited by stray coals from the nursery fireplace. After 11 months and 35,373 miles, *Sunbeam* and the family returned safely home to England—and before long thousands of readers were re-living what became the century's best-known yachting circumnavigation.

Anna Brassey went on many more cruises with her husband, and she wrote three more books about their adventures. In 1887, on a voyage to Australia, she came down with malaria and died aboard *Sunbeam*. She was buried at sea—at 15°50′ S., 110°38′ E., in the Indian Ocean.

Her worldwide popularity helped set an example for similarly hardy yachtswomen. Mary, Duchess of Bedford, for example, cruised up to the Arctic Circle aboard *Sapphire* (pages 120-121). And Empress Eugénie of France, driven into exile by the Franco-Prussian War in 1870 and widowed three years later, spent a good part of her remaining 47 years

William K. Vanderbilt, his family and unidentified guests gather for the camera aboard the yacht Alva during an 1887-1888 Mediterranean cruise. Willie Vanderbilt is in the deck chair at left. Two Vanderbilt children—Consuelo, later Duchess of Marlborough, and Willie Jr.—are in the center. Reclining in the hammock at right is the yacht's namesake, Vanderbilt's wife, Alva. Sprawled on the Oriental carpeting at left is Oliver Belmont, a society bachelor for whom Alva later divorced Willie.

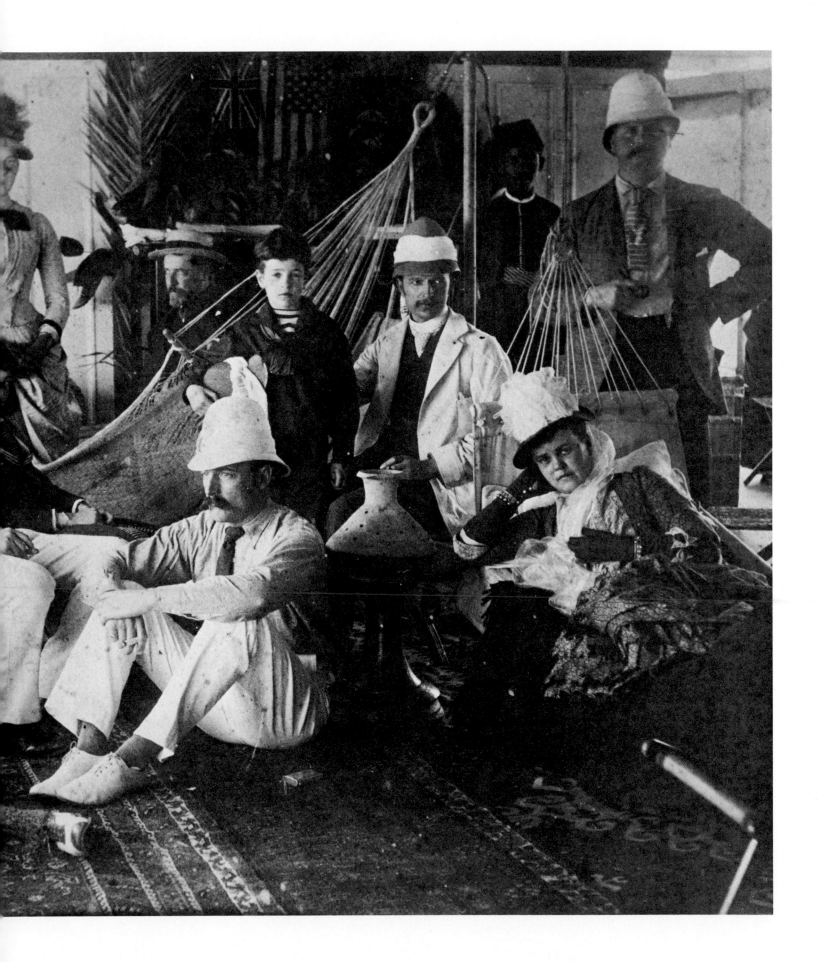

cruising European waters aboard her yacht *Thistle*—often taking the helm during rough weather. "The sea is my element," the Empress wrote. "I should like to live on the sea all the time."

America, too, had its pioneering yachtswomen. A preeminent example was Lucy Carnegie, widow of Thomas Carnegie and sister-in-law of steel tycoon Andrew Carnegie. A woman of independent spirit as well as means, Lucy Carnegie not only matched her fellow yachtsmen afloat— her steel-hulled *Dungeness* was 135 feet long—but also challenged the bastion of their male supremacy: the New York Yacht Club. In 1894, with a minimum of fanfare, Lucy Carnegie asked two friends in the club to put her name up for membership. Thrown into confusion, the membership committee passed the buck by forming another committee to consider her embarrassing proposal—made all the more embarrassing by gleeful accounts in the New York *Herald* that revealed enough details of the discussions to remind members that *Herald* publisher James Gordon Bennett Jr. was a club member.

By March, the special committee had concluded, in Solomon-like fashion, that the New York Yacht Club's rules should be amended to admit yacht-owning women as associate or "Flag Members." This entitled them to fly the club's burgee and use the stations that the club had established along the northeast coast of the U.S. so that mail could be picked up during a cruise; it did not, however, entitle them to enter the sanctum of the club's New York headquarters. Since use of the shore stations was what Mrs. Carnegie really wanted, she found the compromise quite acceptable—as did a number of her peers. The club would have a dozen female flag members by 1910—more than half a century before women were similarly admitted to the Royal Yacht Squadron.

For the most part, the social currents in the world of luxury yachting had developed a wonderful predictability. By the end of the 19th Century, scores of yachtsmen and yachtswomen were following a fixed migratory pattern—to the Riviera in late winter and spring, to the Baltic in the summer, and in August to the yachting mecca, Cowes.

Cowes was Camelot afloat, and its King Arthur was the eldest son of Queen Victoria, an unlikely-looking fat man who nevertheless inspired, as well as presided over, a yachting court. Edward (his mother called him Bertie) had begun to exert his influence as Prince of Wales. Because Victoria treated him as a not-too-astute child and gave him few official duties, he assumed the unofficial role of leader of European society.

It is as a sybarite that Edward VII is most often remembered; he sought out pleasure as obsessively as his father, Prince Albert, had worshipped responsibility. But Edward adopted a rigid pattern for his pastimes. He had a strong streak of punctiliousness, a trait perhaps inherited from his father. His annual procession through the royal playgrounds followed a track as unchanging as the zodiac: the royal estate of Balmoral in Scotland for the autumn shooting season; London during the winter; Paris and Biarritz in the spring, followed by a Mediterranean cruise; Epsom and Ascot for the horse racing in June; a round of country-house visits in the summer, climaxed by Cowes Week in August.

It was at Cowes that Edward's star shone brightest. After he was elect-

The graceful, 256-foot steam yacht below had several owners and names during her 27-year career. But in her years of glory from 1902 to 1914, she was the North Star of Cornelius Vanderbilt III. Vanderbilt (inset), with a beard like that of England's Edward VII, strode the decks in the dress of royal yachtsmen of the day, complete with telescope.

ed commodore of the Royal Yacht Squadron in 1882, the little village on the north shore of the Isle of Wight became the seaside resort not only of the British Royal Family but also of princes and kings from all over Europe, most of them Edward's brothers, cousins and nephews. Among the royal members of the squadron were the Czar of Russia, the Kings of Holland, Sweden, Norway and Belgium, three Prince Henrys (of Russia, Battenberg, and Bourbon), and the thoroughly unpleasant Kaiser Wilhelm II of Germany—whose method of thanking Edward for gaining him membership was to mutter snide remarks about the Prince on the squadron lawn.

During Cowes Week, the roadstead off the Royal Yacht Squadron sprouted a swaying forest of tall masts. Nearly every European head of state had a yacht; even the Vatican commissioned one, christened *Immacolata Concezione*, for Pope Leo XIII. Austria-Hungary had a yacht: Emperor Franz Josef cruised up and down the Danube in a 176-foot paddle-wheeler named *Fantasie*; and when she was dwarfed by other regal vessels, he ordered—from England—a 269-foot paddle-wheeler that he named *Miramar* and brought to Cowes.

At Cowes the sun flashed off dipping oars as visitors were borne from

Jaunts of a doughty Duchess

The traditional decorative role of the 19th Century woman was an anathema to one member of British nobility, the unconventional Duchess of Bedford. She was less interested in the formalities of society than in the rugged joys of exploring, and she led her reluctant spouse, the Duke, on many a merry nautical chase.

In 1901, aboard the chartered *Sapphire (below)*, she was able to satisfy her "ambition to see something of the great frozen North" by sailing to Spitzbergen and beyond, all the way to the Arctic ice pack.

The Duchess was fascinated by the avian life of the northern seas, and in 1903 she bought *Sapphire*, periodically sailing the yacht to the bleak Orkney Islands, off Scotland. On one such expedition she wrote in her diary: "I had an invitation to a party at Buckingham Palace for today, but walked over instead to visit the King of the Birds, viz. the White-tailed Eagle at Waterfalls, North Roe. His Majesty was at home, and gave me a splendid view."

In 1912, the Duchess bought a new, larger yacht, which she also named *Sapphire*, and she continued to rove cold climes until World War I. With the outbreak of hostilities, she offered both the yacht and herself for service. The Royal Navy accepted the yacht but not the Duchess, politely explaining that sea duty was too risky for women.

The 244-foot steam yacht Sapphire lies at anchor in Magdalena Bay during the Duchess' 1901 cruise to Spitzbergen, about 800 miles from the North Pole.

Aboard Sapphire, the Duchess wears her yachting outfit and cradles a favorite doll. This photograph was taken by a guest during the 1901 cruise.

In her bathing suit, the Duchess waves from Spitzbergen's shore. The Duke of Bedford (left), protects his head from the sun with a bandanna, while friend John Findley wears a boater. The Duke eventually found his wife's expeditions too strenuous and stayed home.

Ready to swim, the Duchess (left) lines up on the second Sapphire's deck with cousin Marjorie Russell, friend Janet Tooth (right) and Flora Green (second from right), tutor to the Bedfords' son and a favorite traveling companion.

ship to shore. Steam launches puffed between the yachts, carrying nobles and mere millionaires to afternoon deck parties and evening banquets and balls. Summing up Cowes Week in 1894, the journal *Yachting World* proclaimed: "Society was protuberant, and comprised rank and fashion of all nations. Never have so many yachts graced the beautiful waters of the Solent." Not content with this effusion, the reporter finished with the thought that "every Englishman must be inspired with a feeling of pride when he looks upon this great congress of nations assembled at the chief port of the garden of England."

The imposing figure of Edward could be seen strolling the squadron lawn daily during the season, his yachting kit topped by a white cap. Smoking his ever-present Havana cigar and swinging his ebony walking stick, he escorted one of his favorite lady friends, perhaps Alice Keppel or the actress Lillie Langtry (his mistress in the 1880s)—or occasionally his wife, Alexandra.

In 1892 he commissioned the perfect yacht for his purposes. *Britannia*, built at the then-extravagant cost of £8,000, was a 122-foot cutter fast enough to win many of the Cowes Week races. She also had amenities for the Prince's guests: a deckhouse to shelter ladies from the spray, a commodious main cabin complete with a writing desk and an upright piano, and a ladies' cabin under the afterdeck. The Prince's aging mother reportedly spent her afternoons at a telescope on the Osborne House lawn, spying on *Britannia* in the roadstead to see which of her son's mistresses was on board the yacht with him that day. Victoria rarely ventured out to *Britannia* herself. Perhaps it was just as well, for Bertie's keen-eyed mother probably would have noticed—and certainly would have disapproved of—one memento of her son's liaisons: a royal blue pillow that was adorned by a large red satin flap in the shape of a heart; under the flap was the embroidered inscription: *Avec tout mon coeur*—"with all my heart."

As the years passed, the Prince spent more and more of his time at Cowes aboard his yacht and became quite at home even when her decks were aslant. His aides marveled at Edward's exquisite balance. On one occasion the Prince was sitting in a deck chair reading the morning papers when *Britannia* heeled sharply to the wind. He grasped the companionway coaming just in time, and stood up as chair and papers skidded over the side. At his direction, *Britannia* was jibed and the chair and papers were scooped up. The newspapers were taken to the forecastle to be dried out so that His Highness could finish reading them.

The captains and kings who gathered under Edward's aegis at Cowes made up an almost wildly assorted group—pompous and playful, vain and unassuming, staid and eccentric. A favorite was King Alfonso of Spain, whose spirited bonhomie endeared him to aristocrats and commoners alike. He once put on a memorable display of playfulness when his royal railroad train arrived early at Portsmouth, from which he was to sail across the Spithead to Cowes. Spotting the ample posterior of a stooping railway attendant who was still rolling out the traditional red carpet for him, the King leapfrogged over the astonished porter.

But none of Cowes's royal habitués were more remarkable than Kaiser Wilhelm II of Germany. He was Victoria's grandson and Edward's neph-

Fashions for the afterdeck

Below, an American yachtswoman in blouse and skirt takes the helm; at right, a British beauty affects a naval look.

Nearly as important as the appointments of a luxury yacht at the turn of the century was the outfit one wore when on board. For men, there could be no uncertainty: They donned the standard yachting kit of blue jacket and white slacks. Women of fashion had a wider choice. The options ranged from a flowingly tailored simulacrum of a naval uniform to a considerably more casual blouse and skirt, with a seagoing version of the garden hat firmly tied under the chin.

ew. Willy, as his British kinfolk called him, was a wiry little man with piercing blue eyes, a waxed mustache and a withered left arm. Vain, ambitious, erratic in behavior and often a downright bully, he became Emperor of Germany in 1888, at the age of 29. His mother, Victoria's daughter, made sure he learned to read English; he became absorbed in Alfred T. Mahan's tome *The Influence of Sea Power upon History,* and promptly determined to make Germany a naval power in the British mold. "Our future lies on the water," he announced.

As a preliminary move in that direction, the Kaiser accepted his Uncle Bertie's invitation to join the Royal Yacht Squadron in 1889. He also bought a sailing yacht, but his first cruises on it were less than satisfactory: He discovered that he became uneasy when it heeled to a fresh breeze. Meanwhile, however, he had ordered the construction of a big steamer, assuring his ministers that her prime function would be naval and that she would set the pattern for a Grand Squadron. Four years and 4.5 million marks later, *Hohenzollern* was launched. She was massive: 383 feet long and 3,773 tons. Her engines could produce 9,500 horsepower and speed her along at 21½ knots. She resembled an outsized destroyer. But at her launching, Wilhelm surprised everybody by announcing that she was now his royal yacht.

The Kaiser delighted in his new plaything. He had a great imperial eagle painted over her prow, and he outfitted the yacht with luxurious appointments. Cruising aboard *Hohenzollern* in the Baltic and to England, often escorted by a pack of warships, he fired off orders to his government and daydreamed of future German naval triumphs.

A typical Wilhelm performance was his arrival for Cowes Week in 1894. *Hohenzollern,* 83 feet longer than *Victoria and Albert II,* moved grandly up the roadstead, dipping her imperial standard at the masthead as she passed Willy's grandmother at Osborne House. Amid ceremonial firing of cannon, the great white yacht rounded to her mooring within two minutes of her scheduled time.

Willy was almost uncontrollably jealous of his uncle's social success with Cowes Week. He referred to the Prince of Wales as "the old peacock," and he found Edward's retinue dissolute. No doubt he enjoyed the gibes of some blue-water sailors who called the squadron lawn a "marine Madame Tussaud's" and nicknamed the Kaiser's portly uncle "Tum-Tum." Nevertheless the Kaiser copied the Prince's yachting outfit. He aped the aristocrats around him, dropping his g's and repeating the glib bons mots, usually getting them wrong. He strutted about the lawn, fancying slights even when there were none. Despite his best efforts to fit into the yachting and social scene, he sensed a barrier. In the deadly phrase of one member of the squadron, the Kaiser was "not quite a gentleman."

So Willy decided that if he could not truly join them he would beat them. He established his own yachting festival, Kiel Week—held at the Baltic resort in June—and invited the same royalty and aristocracy. Few accepted—and even fewer returned for a second time after being overwhelmed by brass bands, constant cannon fire, goose-stepping guards of honor and medal-bedecked officers saluting and heel-clicking at an unending series of formal banquets and receptions. The Kaiser could not

Aboard his royal yacht Osborne II, Edward, Prince of Wales, sits in a basket chair for a formal portrait with his wife, Alexandra (center), and their children (from left) Maud, Louise, Albert Victor, George and (seated on the deck) Victoria.

understand why this flashy display proved less attractive than the gentle garden receptions and deck parties of Cowes.

Understandably, Edward fretted over his nephew's souring of the cream of European royalty at Cowes. To a German friend he put it politely: "The Regatta used to be my favourite relaxation; but since the Emperor has been in command here, it's nothing but a nuisance." He became less and less interested in this unpleasant family scene.

Then, in 1901, Queen Victoria died at Osborne House. She had commissioned a new steam yacht, the 380-foot-long *Victoria and Albert III*, and had made so many suggestions for additions and improvements that the completed yacht was top-heavy; when eased out of drydock in May 1899, the vessel tilted over at a 24° angle and was righted only with difficulty. It took two years to correct the yacht's balance, and Victoria never used her. At her state funeral, her catafalque was carried to the mainland from the Isle of Wight aboard the tender *Alberta;* the royal mourners followed aboard *Victoria and Albert II.*

Now that he had finally succeeded to the throne at the age of 59, Edward VII took his royal duties more seriously. He also felt obliged to be more magnanimous to his nephew the Kaiser. In 1904 the King made the grand gesture of urging his fellow yachtsmen to attend the Kaiser's regatta at Kiel. Kiel Week that year was the first that could be called a success.

Still, the occasion was marred by the Kaiser's choice of British yachting companions. One was the flamboyant Earl of Lonsdale, a favorite of Willy's and known to Royal Yacht Squadron members as "the yellow earl" because of the color of his fleet of carriages and automobiles. Making a ceremonial entrance at Kiel Week aboard his big steamer *Finlandia,* Lonsdale sauntered ashore clad in striped trousers and a yellow waistcoat over a silk shirt and hunting stock, chewing a long cigar and sporting a wide-brimmmed Panama hat. Handing his suitcase to the startled admiral who had come to welcome him, Lonsdale strode past a guard of honor lined up in full regalia and entered the clubhouse. The other visiting British yachtsmen winced at his performance; it was almost as bad form as Lonsdale's earlier insistence that the painter of the official portrait of squadron members place him in the front row with the royal and elder members. The artist complied, only to have the outraged senior members demand that the earl be painted out and moved to a less prominent spot.

The distinction between Lord Lonsdale and his fellow squadron members was largely lost on the American yachtsmen now swarming to England. They were fascinated by what seemed to them a quaintly attractive scene, and their hosts in turn were intrigued by the Americans' reaction. Vita Sackville-West pinpointed the phenomenon in her novel *The Edwardians.* Describing a visiting American millionaire, the novel's Lady Roehampton remonstrates with a snobbish young Briton: "But, darling, you don't appreciate the *freshness* of his mind; we all appear to him like a lot of old waxworks; he told me so himself; such an amusing idea, I think." Indeed, she points out, when the rich visitor spotted one of the British country estates "he wanted to buy the whole house and move it brick by brick to America." As *The Edwardians* warned, "The Ameri-

A raffish gallery of Cowes's elite

As is the case today, the Royal Yacht Squadron's turn-of-the-century membership included some of the most prestigious figures of Great Britain, yet one could hardly guess this from the evidence of the caricatures shown here. They are the work of the Earl of Albemarle, a conservative pillar of British society who possessed a puckish natural talent for portraiture.

Wealth, a yacht exceeding 30 tons, and impeccable lineage or high achievement (preferably both) were the chief qualifications for membership in the exclusive squadron. However, the noblemen, Members of Parliament, and distinguished scientists and explorers who were admitted to the club soon discovered that, when the irrepressible earl was on the prowl, their dignity was far from safe within the protective walls of the squadron's squat fortress at Cowes. Still, such was the portraitist's wit and acuteness of eye that the most eminent members considered it an honor to be caricatured by Albemarle—and even to be pilloried on the clubhouse walls, from which this gallery has been selected.

Zanily smothered in wind-blown whiskers in this portrayal by Albemarle, Lord Crawford was one of Britain's most prominent astronomers.

The *Albemarle* portrait that some members considered his best is this one of Captain Henry Denison. Denison spent most of his time sitting in a chair on the squadron lawn commenting on the foibles of fellow members.

Deceptively serene in the earl's portrait, Lord Dunraven was a quick-tempered and brilliant yachtsman who wrote technical treatises on navigation.

Albemarle's rumpled Sir Allen Young, his telescope under his arm, hardly flattered the former clipper-ship captain. One of England's greatest navigators, he led five Arctic expeditions and helped in the organization of the Chinese Navy.

cans were discovering Europe far more rapidly than the Europeans had discovered America.''

The acquisitive, go-getting United States yachtsmen were surprised to find that the prestigious Royal Yacht Squadron clubhouse had no locker rooms, no showers, no dock and not even a bar. Yet the members' yachts were bastions of elegance: The cabins and staterooms were resplendent with understated grandeur, and evening dress was the custom for dinner. When the American yacht designer L. Francis Herreshoff was invited aboard a British yacht to inspect her seagoing qualities, he was astonished by her fine interior cabinetwork and Parisian upholstery. Spending the night on the vessel, he found that he could not even sit up to read in bed, because he kept slipping down between the silk sheets.

The Yankee yachtsmen and their wives were delighted by the scene on the squadron lawn as the King paraded about with his retinue of handsome ladies in long silk gowns and enormous, floppy hats. They tirelessly angled for invitations to dine or take tea aboard the yachts of royalty and nobility. Cowes seemed to the transatlantic visitors an enchanted world, shining by day with brass, mahogany and the flash of white oars, and dancing by night on black waters lighted by soft lanterns and sudden eruptions of fireworks.

The Americans enjoyed Kiel Week almost as much, partly because Kaiser Wilhelm took a liking to these New World yachtsmen, though he was sometimes bemused by their frank and open display of wealth. The most impressive yacht at Kiel Week in 1904 was financier Morton F. Plant's gleaming schooner *Ingomar*. Inspecting the vessel during the regatta, the Kaiser was particularly taken with the visitors' book, which had a silver cover. Invited to sign it, he muttered, ''Dear, dear, even a silver book. How rich you Americans are!''

The Kaiser's interest in yachting, while obviously genuine, involved an ulterior motive. ''The Germans are not a yachting nation,'' his brother Prince Henry explained to British yachtsman Brooke Heckstall-Smith, adding that they know ''nothing about navies or the sea. Half of them have never seen the sea. But if they go to the seaside for their holidays and read about the Emperor's yacht and so forth, and wealthy merchants who know nothing of the sport try to become sportsmen and yachtsmen to please the Emperor, then it stirs up the interest in the seafaring pursuits and we can get money for the Navy.'' British yachtsmen, many with strong ties to the Royal Navy, were well aware of the Kaiser's expansionist ambitions. Indeed, many of the visiting German yachtsmen in the years before World War I were suspected by their British hosts of being spies. But it was considered unpardonably rude to say so.

Another yachtsman entitled to his suspicions concerning the Kaiser was Nicholas II of Russia, who was married to one of Victoria's granddaughters. In marked contrast to Wilhelm, the Czar was gentle and withdrawn, a family man. His first yacht was the 337-foot *Pole Star*, launched by his father, Alexander III, in 1888. But Nicholas decided that he wanted more room, so he ordered a second yacht, this one a monster at 420 feet and 4,334 tons. Christened *Standart*, she was launched in 1895. She was larger and handsomer than *Hohenzollern*, much to the Kaiser's

The elegant seasonal itinerary

The wealthiest yachtsmen of the late 19th and early 20th Centuries knew not only the best way to travel but the best places to go. Following a rigid social calendar, the largest yachts cruised from the United States to Europe in an annual pilgrimage.

An early summer attraction was the genteel grandeur of Oyster Bay (*below*), whose Seawanhaka Yacht Club's members included J. P. Morgan, William K. Vanderbilt and President Theodore Roosevelt. Even larger flotillas gathered at Newport (*next page*) for regattas, polo and tennis matches, and all-night balls in seaside palaces that moved a visiting Russian Grand Duke to exclaim, ''Is this really America?''

By late summer the elegant action had shifted to the royal regattas at Cowes and Kiel. And even during the winter the floating festivals continued, in Monte Carlo (*page 132*), where the yachts were strung with flowers as well as flags, and in Venice where, 10 centuries after it had all begun with the Doges, aerial fireworks were reflected in the evening waters, and the melodies from special music barges echoed down the long canals. By springtime, perhaps after a Caribbean cruise, the big yachts were being refurbished to set out on their sybaritic circle all over again.

Shielded by her parasol from the Oyster Bay sun, a gentlewoman prepares to board a yacht in 1905. That same year, Seawanhaka Club member Theodore Roosevelt chose Long Island's Oyster Bay for a diplomatic meeting, aboard the presidential yacht Mayflower, that led to the end of the Russo-Japanese War.

Flag-bedecked yachts decorate England's Solent (below) during Cowes Week in 1909. At left, Kiel regatta, which was held on the Baltic Sea, attrac a forest of masts in 1912.

Newport dowagers (right) watch a regatta from the grassy slope of Castle Hill in the 1890s, while liveried attendants wait in the carriages to drive them home to their million-dollar "cottages."

In the foreground at left, Prince Albert
of Monaco's yacht, Princesse Alice, lies at
anchor in the harbor at Monte Carlo.
Below, the French imperial yacht L'Aigle
moors in Venice' Grand Canal.

pique. *Standart* had long lines sweeping aft from her gold-leafed figurehead. Her hull was black, her two stacks gleaming white except at the top, where black paint hid the inevitable soot. The three masts were used only for rows of flags on state visits.

Every June the Czar, his wife, Alexandra, and their five children cruised for two weeks along the coast of Finland. Although *Standart* was usually escorted on these cruises by several torpedo boats and courier vessels relaying government papers to and from St. Petersburg, no officials or security guards were permitted aboard the yacht. The children were kept under the protective eye of hand-picked seamen, whom the Czar rewarded at the end of the cruise with gold watches. Sometimes Nicholas and the family would be ferried ashore to walk in the woods or play tennis on courts owned by local noblemen. A ship's band stood by to entertain the Czar in the evenings; there was also a balalaika orchestra in case the family was in the mood for folk music. Afterward, evening prayers would be said in the yacht's chapel before the family retired, far from the turmoil and assassination plots back home.

During the summer of 1907 the Czar and his family were on their annual cruise when *Standart* suddenly grounded on a rock and began to settle quickly. As the Czarina herded the children and maids into the boats and gathered her jewels and icons in a bed sheet, the Czar calmly studied the yacht's subsiding water line. *Standart* had been constructed with watertight compartments, and the Czar was intent on seeing how well they worked. He estimated that *Standart* had 20 more minutes above water; but to his surprise and gratification the buoyant compartments stabilized the yacht, and she remained afloat. The family was taken to the smaller *Pole Star*, aboard which they finished the cruise while *Standart* was undergoing repairs.

While the Czar preferred to use his yachts for quiet, idyllic vacations, Kaiser Wilhelm had a penchant for indulging in a highly personal kind of waterborne diplomacy. One of his forays concerned France. His pugnacious ways had made him unpopular in Paris, and he did not further endear himself to the Third Republic by openly courting the friendship of Napoleon III's widow, Empress Eugénie. During the summer of 1907, Eugénie was aboard *Thistle* in the North Sea. On July 25 the Empress and her yachting party steamed into the harbor of Bergen, Norway, to find it jammed with German cruisers awaiting the arrival of the Kaiser. One of her guests suggested turning away and going to another harbor. The Empress' Bonapartist friends had no desire to meet the German head of state, since defeat by Germany had brought their regime down. Eugénie, however, felt that flight would be more embarrassing. She had met the Kaiser once before; he had tried in his clumsy way to charm her, and she did not want to snub him.

Thistle anchored amid the cruisers, "looking like a miserable little prisoner of war," wrote Isabel Vesey, Eugénie's traveling companion. At 11:30 p.m., *Hohenzollern*, escorted by a cruiser and a gunboat, steamed into the harbor, and despite the hour, the German cruisers fired an echoing salute. Eugénie had gone to her stateroom and to bed, but she was called out to greet the Kaiser's aide-de-camp, who had climbed aboard her yacht. Would it be convenient for the Emperor to pay his respects next morning, the aide inquired—and what should His Majesty wear?

Eugénie suggested 11 a.m. and civilian clothes. The next morning it was raining heavily, and *Thistle*'s crew spread awnings above the deck. The Kaiser, punctual to the minute, "skipped up the ladder," according to Miss Vesey's report, "and he and the Empress went through the formality of embracing."

Eugénie presented her party, and Kaiser Wilhelm cordially shook hands with them, ignoring or pretending to ignore the sour looks of the French ladies. The Empress and the Kaiser then went below to one of the cabins, and her guests grudgingly made small talk with the stiff-necked German officers. Eugénie and Willy remained below-decks for more than two hours, while the Germans ran out of French phrases, the French yachting guests became more impatient and the rain thrummed on the canvas awning. When finally the royal pair emerged, the Kaiser insisted on shaking hands with everyone again before he bounded down the ladder to his tender. Miss Vesey wrote home that he appeared effusive and awkward, "not at all imposing but very determined-looking." He wore, she acidly added, "too many rings, a bracelet and bright yellow shoes."

Eugénie gave her friends a summary of her discussion with the Kaiser. He expressed a wish to visit Paris, where he was not welcome. He was bitter toward the British Royal Family, whose members had not given him a memento of his grandmother Victoria after her death. Eugénie had shown him about the interior of the yacht, which he praised, characteristically adding that all of *Thistle* could be fitted into one cabin of *Hohenzollern*, then laughing to indicate that this was a joke. Miss Vesey added, evidently in some surprise, that "as a matter of fact, the Empress rather likes him." On departure the next morning the Kaiser ordered the French flag flown by his fleet and his sailors ranged on deck. He did not know that his gesture of respect was lost on Eugénie: It was 7 a.m. and she was still asleep.

Nicholas II was also a target of the Kaiser's yachting diplomacy. He and Wilhelm met aboard their yachts in June 1912. *Hohenzollern* and *Standart* anchored alongside each other at Reval (now Tallinn), Estonia. The Kaiser played with the youngest Romanov daughter, Anastasia, and presented expensive gifts to the rest of the family. On the last day, Wilhelm held a morning reception at which the naval officers consumed 60 bottles of champagne in an hour and a half. The Kaiser and the Czar never saw each other again.

That summer British yachtsman Brooke Heckstall-Smith noted an even more martial air than usual at Kiel Week: "Aeroplanes were soaring overhead at a vast height, like peregrine falcons on the wing; a noisy, enormous Zeppelin, a ponderous, unsightly object, was humming over the fjord. In the harbour in a double line were moored the German fleet of dreadnoughts and battleships, with many submarines, destroyers and torpedo craft." Ashore, bands played constantly while the German Army goose-stepped past. A German admiral confronted Heckstall-Smith at breakfast one morning during the regatta and, ignoring the protests from his fellow hosts, predicted that this would be the last Kiel Week in which the British would play a leading part, because a continental war was

Kaiser Wilhelm II could pose benignly on board his yacht Hohenzollern with his three grandsons (above) or make an aggressive display with the huge steamer. Designed as a naval vessel, Hohenzollern presents a stark contrast to the graceful silhouettes of nearby pleasure craft during one of the Kaiser's visits to Cowes.

inevitable, and it would give Germany dominance over all of Europe.

The Kaiser, everyone knew, was busily forging alliances in hopes of dominating a volatile Europe. A major element in his plan, an alliance with the Austro-Hungarian Empire, was suddenly endangered in the summer of 1914—during Kiel Week. The Kaiser was presiding over his regatta from *Hohenzollern* on the afternoon of June 28 when a Navy launch chugged out with a message. Wilhelm waved it off. But the launch officer would not retreat. He folded the message, tucked it into a cigarette case and tossed it aboard the royal yacht. A sailor picked it up and presented it to the Kaiser.

In full naval regalia, Russia's Czar Nicholas II (left) converses with Kaiser Wilhelm II, his German counterpart and cousin by marriage. At the turn of the century, Europe's yachting monarchs, many related by blood or marriage, met often and engaged in a spirited rivalry over who could build the largest yacht.

Wilhelm read the message: Archduke Franz Ferdinand, the heir to the Austro-Hungarian throne and an ally of the Kaiser, had been assassinated at Sarajevo. Wilhelm muttered, "Now I've got to begin all over again." He abruptly canceled the rest of the festivities planned for Kiel Week and went back to Berlin.

One month later, on Saturday, August 1, many of the same European yachtsmen were gathering in the Solent for Cowes Week. Launches ran like water bugs through the forest of tall masts, bearing guests to the deck parties in the anchorage. The squadron lawn presented its annual tapestry of blue serge jackets and white dresses. But tension was in the air. Two days earlier the newspapers had reported that England's Home Fleet had gone to sea under sealed orders. On Friday, Lord Ormonde, commodore of the Royal Yacht Squadron, had received a telegram from King George V, who had succeeded to the throne on Edward VII's death in 1910; the telegram expressed regrets that His Majesty could not come to Cowes. The Kaiser had already sent his regrets as well, but his popular naval aide and yachtsman, Admiral von Eisendecker, had arrived as a guest of the commodore, and Prince Henry of Prussia was expected shortly. Prince Henry never arrived; and on Saturday Admiral von Eisendecker quietly disappeared.

At the request of some anxious squadron members, Commodore Ormonde messaged Buckingham Palace to ask if the King felt that the Cowes regatta should proceed—a diplomatic way of ascertaining how His Majesty gauged the threat of war. On Sunday the reply came: "The King thinks the regatta should be postponed."

Like many of their crewmen, squadron members in the Naval Reserve were by now receiving the news directly: They were recalled to active duty. An even more ominous sign, in the opinion of a few members, was the squadron's decision to stop cashing their checks. Lord Albemarle wrote: "I looked upon this as the most evil of omens." (He could, however, take comfort in the fact that he had had the foresight to withdraw £200 from his London bank before coming down to Cowes.)

By Tuesday, August 4, Belgium had been invaded, and the next day England was at war with Germany. Already the Cowes pleasure fleet had thinned out, the remaining members temporarily dining free so that the squadron could get rid of the food stocked up for Cowes Week. Only a few were on hand for the club's annual dinner on Tuesday evening; but tradition was upheld in a telegraphed toast to the King: "Deeply regretting Your Majesty's absence for reasons which commend themselves to every Englishman, the Royal Yacht Squadron drinks to Your Majesty's health and lifelong prosperity."

Over the ramparts of the squadron's castle, the Royal Navy's white ensign with its St. George's cross fluttered, dipped and then dropped down the flagstaff. The privilege of flying the ensign, which had been granted to the squadron 80 years earlier by William IV, reverted exclusively to the Navy in wartime. The dousing of the ensign signaled the end of an era of waterborne luxury. With skeleton crews, the yachts at Cowes slipped their moorings and headed across the Solent to Southampton, where their aristocratic owners worked in shirt sleeves on greasy wharves to secure them to shore.

The Romanovs' summer refuge

For Russia's Czar Nicholas II and his family, the 420-foot royal yacht *Standart* provided an escape from the routine cares of monarchy—and even more from threats of assassination in the early-20th Century atmosphere of palace intrigue and revolutionary fever. Every June, the Royal Family cruised the Baltic, taking tea in wicker chairs under white canvas awnings, worshipping in the yacht's chapel and reading in mahogany-paneled drawing rooms. They enjoyed an easy informality with the crew; often the yacht's officers joined the family at the imperial dining table.

Although the Czar barred all government ministers from the yacht, affairs of state could not be fully fended off. Daily courier boats brought dispatches from St. Petersburg. And the ever-present escort of naval craft, as well as a platoon of marines aboard the yacht, was a constant reminder of lurking political peril.

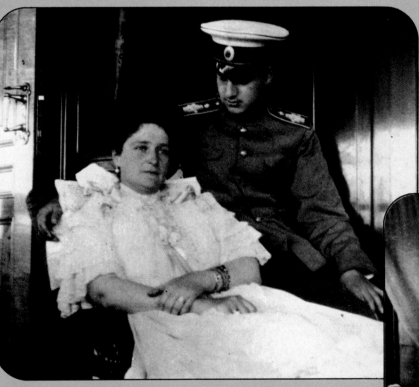

Crippling sciatica confined Czarina Alexandra to deck chairs aboard Standart. Her companion in this picture is Grand Duke Dmitri, her husband's cousin.

The youngest Romanovs, nine-year-old Anastasia and seven-year-old Alexis, cavort for the camera in the children's dining room during a 1910 cruise.

In a 1914 photograph taken by Alexandra, Nicholas II is resplendent in naval uniform. He was devoted to yachting despite recurrent seasickness.

Czarevitch Alexis nearly always wore a Russian sailor's uniform in the summer, whether aboard Standart or ashore.

The four Grand Duchesses—from left, Maria, Olga, Anastasia and Tatiana— assemble for an impromptu portrait during a cruise aboard Standart in 1909.

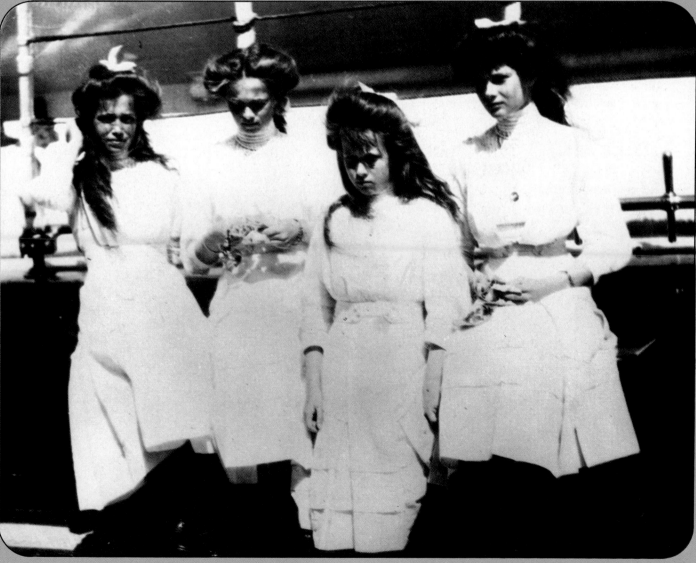

The Royal Yacht Squadron's castle served as a temporary naval base, and 34 members' yachts were designated as naval vessels. Most of them did patrol duty; one sank a German submarine. Sir Thomas Lipton's *Erin*, escorting his fourth America's Cup challenger to the United States when war broke out, ducked into Bermuda, then accompanied the racing vessel to New York and returned across the Atlantic. Lipton lent *Erin* to the Red Cross, and she ferried doctors and nurses to the Austrian front. Later the Admiralty took her over and put her on patrol duty. *Erin* was sunk by a U-boat while she was rushing to the aid of a torpedoed cruiser in the Mediterranean.

The British royal yacht *Britannia* was laid up for the duration. The Czar's *Standart* took the Romanov family, then cruising off the Finnish coast, home to Russia—and to their deaths in the Russian Revolution. For years afterward there were rumors that Nicholas and his family had escaped aboard a ship, presumably *Standart*, and were cruising the White Sea, endlessly awaiting a call for return of the monarchy. *Standart* wound up as a Soviet minelayer. As for the Kaiser's *Hohenzollern*, she sat out World War I and was broken up for scrap in 1923. In 1913, Wilhelm had ordered a new *Hohenzollern* even larger than the first. Her unfinished hull lay in a Stettin shipyard during the War, and it too was dismantled in 1923.

When the United States went to war in 1917, so did many American yachtsmen. Commodore Vanderbilt's great-grandson Harold Vanderbilt commissioned a patrol boat, was put in command of her by the Navy and went searching for enemy submarines. J. P. Morgan Jr. sold his father's third *Corsair* to the Navy for one dollar. Her paneling was stripped away, and enough bunks were crowded into her once commodious staterooms to take care of 12 officers and 122 men, most of whom were young naval reservists from Princeton. She was armed with depth charges and deck guns and sent off across the Atlantic on convoy duty. At Saint Nazaire, France, *Corsair* joined a small fleet of other converted yachts that had been assigned to patrols. She later recrossed the Atlantic a number of times on convoy duty, and was credited with rescuing crewmen from several torpedoed ships. At the end of the War, *Corsair* was returned to Morgan. He then restored her yachting comforts and converted her coal bunkers to oil tanks—in time for her to serve as flagship of the New York Yacht Club. The junior Morgan, like his father, had been elected commodore.

The New York Yacht Club had reacted to World War I by canceling the honorary membership they had given the Kaiser. An American yachtsman named Wilson Marshall also did his part when he donated to the Red Cross a cup that had been awarded by the Kaiser before the War. In a series of auctions, it brought some $125,000 from patriotic purchasers, who then returned the cup to the Red Cross. A final fund-raising event was held in New York's Metropolitan Opera House. Before an audience that had paid five dollars each for admission, and with President Woodrow Wilson in attendance, yachtsman Marshall dramatically shattered the Kaiser's cup with a sledge hammer. The trophy turned out not to be solid gold as the Kaiser had claimed, but thinly gold-plated pewter worth about $35.

Sir Thomas Lipton joins six Red Cross nurses for a patriotic picture (top) after turning his luxury steam yacht Erin into a World War I hospital transport. An irrepressible partygiver, Lipton hosted a masquerade during one Mediterranean passage, and the nurses dressed as members of a Turkish harem (bottom).

A revolutionary vessel for the Czar

In the late 1870s, Czar Alexander II expressed a wish for a new yacht to cruise the Black Sea. The result was a marvel of technological innovation, majestic scale and luxurious appointments—and one of the most unusual vessels ever launched. *Livadia* was the brain child of Vice Admiral Alexander Popov, who modeled it on his own designs for circular, floating gun platforms—wide, shallow-draft vessels that were relatively stable under the weight of massive artillery pieces. Popov reasoned that a similar design for the royal yacht would reduce rolling (and royal seasickness) while supporting capacious quarters.

Livadia—seen here and on the following four pages in architectural diagrams—emerged with startling dimen-

sions. She was 235 feet long and 153 across the beam, more than half as wide as her length. The 11,000-ton, ellipsoidal yacht towered 36 feet above the surface, yet drew only six and a half feet of water.

The Glasgow shipbuilders of John Elder & Co. rushed *Livadia* to completion in less than a year, but Alexander was assassinated shortly before the delivery of the yacht to Sevastopol. His heirs found *Livadia* a dubious legacy. Although she proved stable enough in calm waters, she disappointed Popov's expectations by rolling violently in choppy seas. In consequence, the novel yacht was never used by any of the Romanov family; after years of idling, she was broken up for scrap in 1926.

At the water line Livadia's bulbous hull widened into ledges that, by means of pillars, supported platforms extending from the upper deck like the veranda of a royal dacha. The yacht had three smokestacks side by side; only the starboard one is visible here.

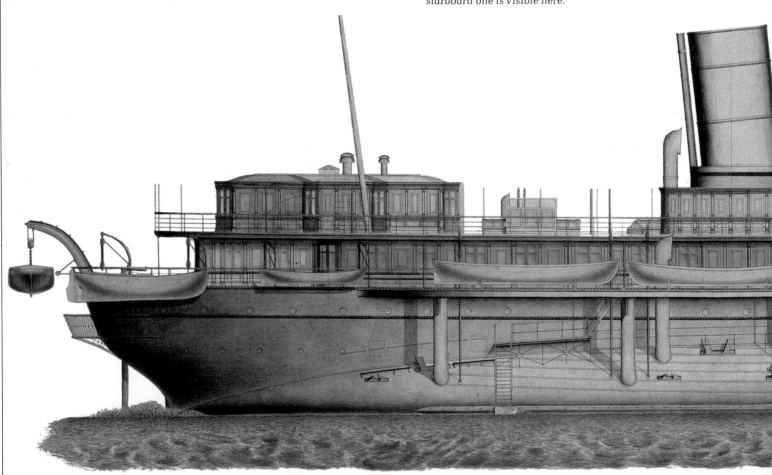

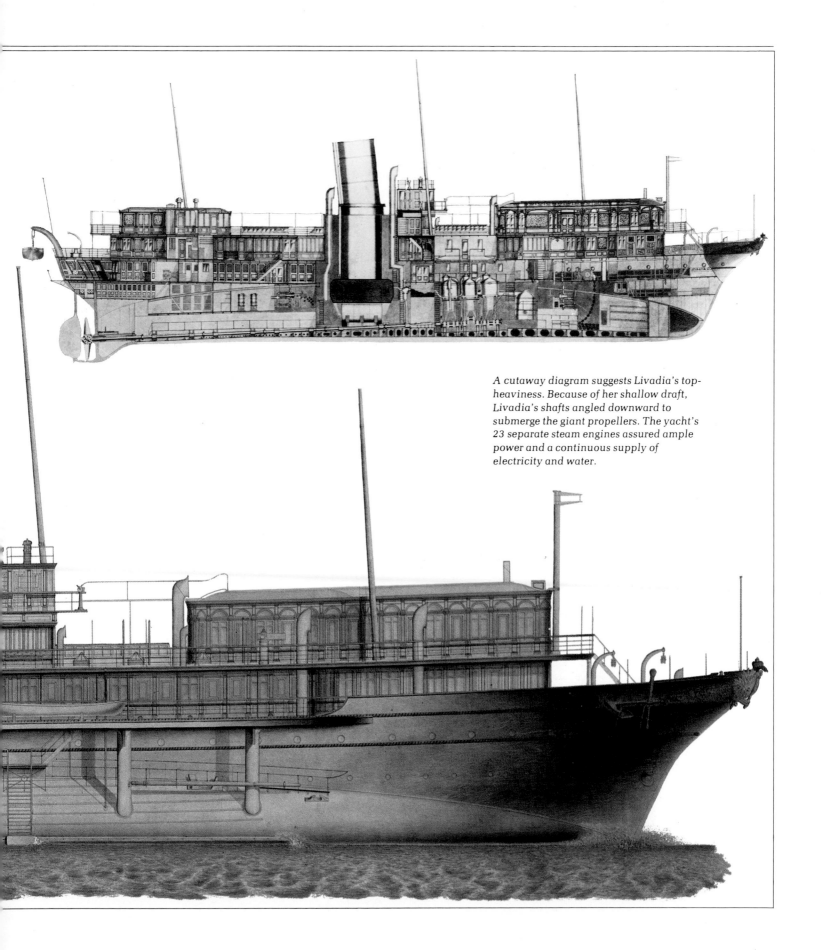

A cutaway diagram suggests Livadia's top-heaviness. Because of her shallow draft, Livadia's shafts angled downward to submerge the giant propellers. The yacht's 23 separate steam engines assured ample power and a continuous supply of electricity and water.

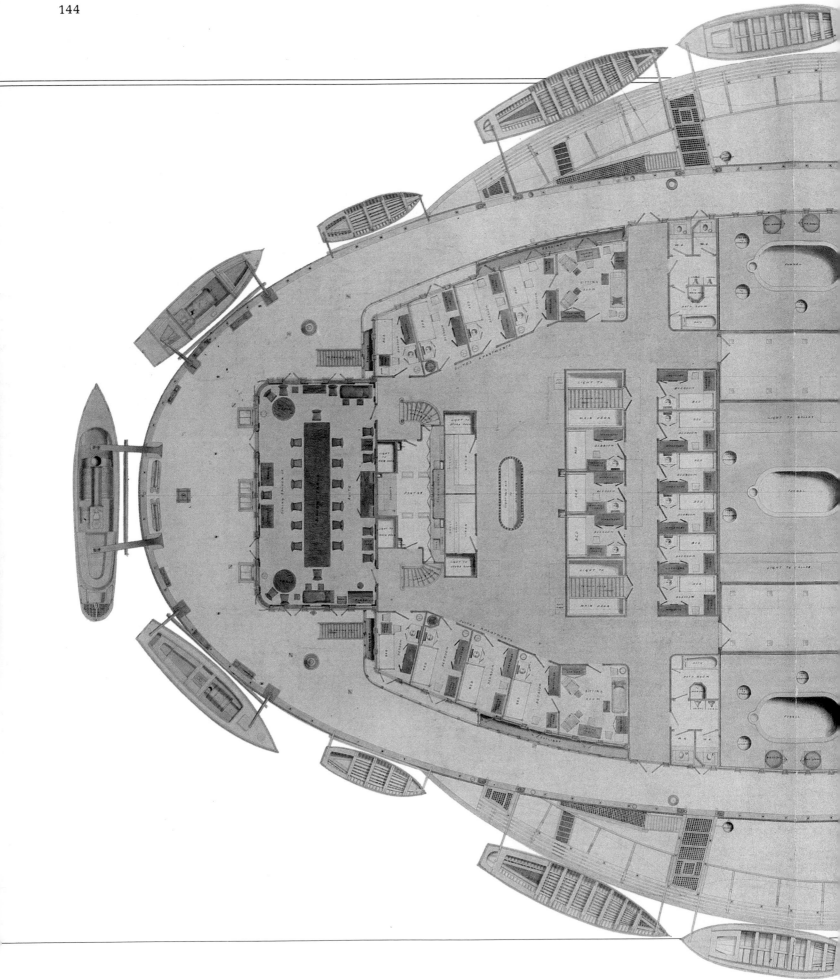

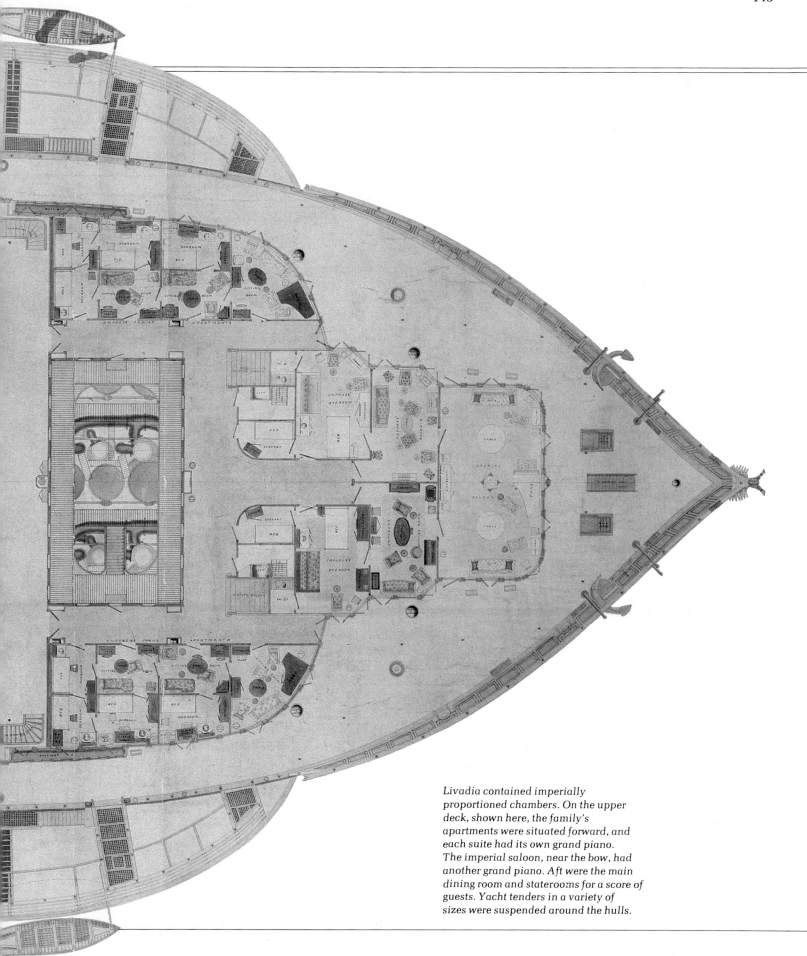

Livadia contained imperially proportioned chambers. On the upper deck, shown here, the family's apartments were situated forward, and each suite had its own grand piano. The imperial saloon, near the bow, had another grand piano. Aft were the main dining room and staterooms for a score of guests. Yacht tenders in a variety of sizes were suspended around the hulls.

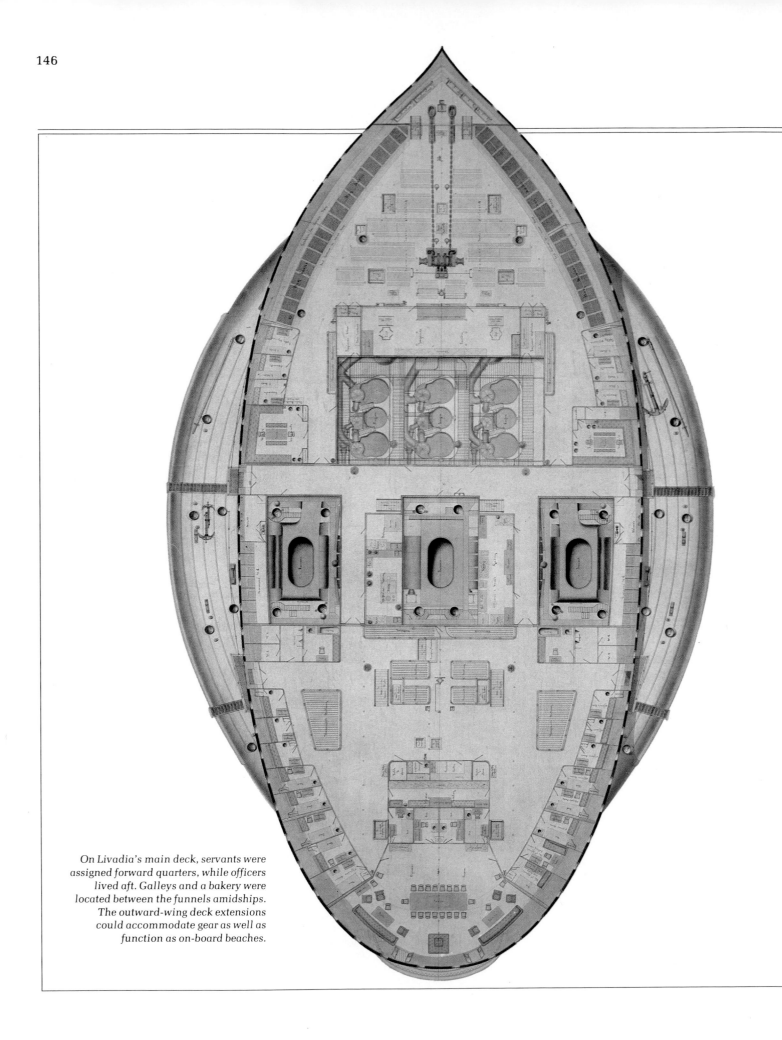

On Livadia's main deck, servants were
assigned forward quarters, while officers
lived aft. Galleys and a bakery were
located between the funnels amidships.
The outward-wing deck extensions
could accommodate gear as well as
function as on-board beaches.

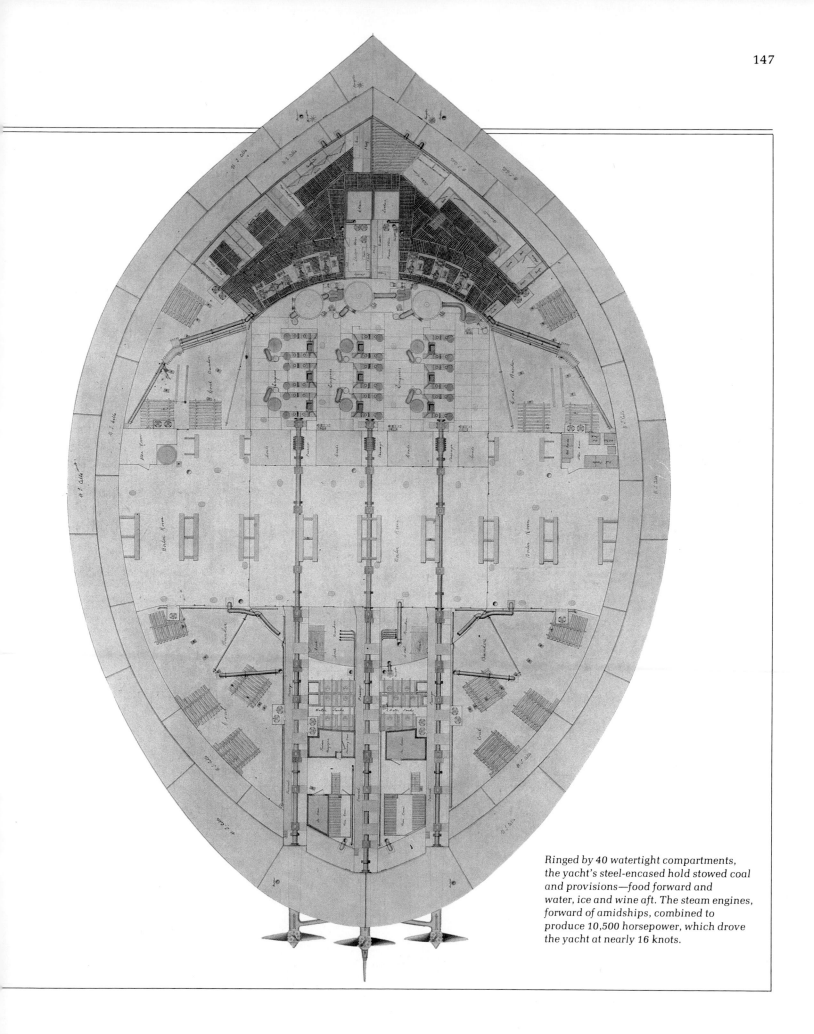

Ringed by 40 watertight compartments, the yacht's steel-encased hold stowed coal and provisions—food forward and water, ice and wine aft. The steam engines, forward of amidships, combined to produce 10,500 horsepower, which drove the yacht at nearly 16 knots.

Chapter 5

A final burst of excess

orld War I had a devastating effect on the yachtsmen of Cowes. Many British yachts were sold during the War at distress prices to newly rich yachtsmen in the neutral Scandinavian countries. The War also wiped out much of England's aristocracy: Thousands of titled young men died in the trenches or went down in warships of the Royal Navy.

The British yachtsmen who began to appear at Cowes after the War resembled their American visitors: Most were self-made men or the sons of such men. Many sported titles awarded, like Sir Thomas Lipton's, for service to the government or for charitable activity—Lord Waring was an ex-shopkeeper, Sir Howard Frank a real-estate magnate, Sir William Berry a newspaper owner, Sir Charles Allom an architect.

A number of these Cowes habitués seemed decidedly less at home on a yacht than the few remaining veteran sailors were. Sir William Portal, heir to a railroad fortune, spent most of the summer season on his comfortably appointed *Valdora*, but disliked sailing when there was much wind, explaining that he liked an upright position. Herbert Weld was better known as an archeologist and naturalist than as a yachtsman; invariably his first move on coming aboard his yacht *Lulworth* was to retire below with *The Times*. Returning to deck after the yacht was under way and was heeling sharply, he would exclaim, "Hello! We've started!"

Many a new millionaire, squadron leaders complained, assumed that when he had bought a yacht and hired a captain he was a fully accredited yachtsman. Often there was reason to doubt the strength of his ties to the sport. As evidence, the old guard cited a newly titled tycoon who surveyed the Solent from a launch with his captain. Pointing to a large cutter, he said, "Brown, that's the *Shamrock* over there, isn't it?"

"Yes, that's 'er, Sir Walter," the captain replied.

"And wouldn't that be the *White Heather* just astern of her, Brown?"

Brown acknowledged that Sir Walter was correct.

Sir Walter said, "But damned if I can recognize the white cutter," and asked who owned her.

After a pained pause, the captain replied, "You do, Sir Walter."

The new look at Cowes was particularly distressing to the squadron's most prominent member, King George V, who had succeeded to the throne upon Edward VII's death in 1910. Unlike his father, he did not enjoy the social life ashore. Instead of strolling the squadron lawn, he preferred clapping on his brimless sailor's cap and going for a brisk sail aboard the royal cutter *Britannia*—and the stronger the wind the better.

Queen Mary gamely joined her husband on some of these expeditions, smiling regally to the subjects who flocked around the royal yacht, and then ducking below. But one sail in the summer of 1923 was too much for her. In a howling gale, with Queen Mary huddled below and King

One of the glories of modern-day yachting, Marjorie Post's 316-foot Sea Cloud—launched in 1931 and originally named Hussar—combined the beauty of a square-rigger with the efficiency and comfort supplied by four diesel engines and a gyroscope stabilizer.

George dashing about the deck helping haul the lines, *Britannia's* jib topsail broke loose. Its steel halyard thrashed about like a gigantic snake, whistling around the mast and banging a tattoo on the deck. Everyone, including the King, pitched in to make it fast, ducking to avoid being decapitated by one of its murderous loops. When it was finally secured, the King shouted to the skipper, "Send someone below to find out how the Queen is." A sailor went below and soon came back on deck.

"Well, how is Her Majesty?" asked the King.

The sailor doffed his sou'wester and seemed at a loss for words.

"Well, what did she say," His Majesty shouted. "Speak up!"

The seaman gulped, stammered and then answered. " Her Majesty said—' Never again, she's damned if she will!' "

George V was more interested in the speed than in the comforts of *Britannia*, and his spending habits differed greatly from those of his father. A guest aboard the yacht was amazed to be offered a halved cigar after dinner. A London jeweler was given a similar lesson in royal parsimony when he submitted samples for a gold yachting trophy to be awarded by the sovereign. George selected a cup—but sent word that he could not afford its lid as well. He often boasted that the main saloon of the *Britannia* still had its original carpet. After the skipper spilled ink on the carpet, the King refused to order a replacement, instead giving instructions for cleaning the carpet when the yachting season ended.

A refreshing glimpse of life aboard a royal yacht with George V was provided by a yachtsman who visited Cowes near the end of George's reign. The visitor was Gerard B. Lambert, the sort of sailor-gentleman George V could expect to like. Lambert had made his fortune with a mouthwash, but his lineage was impeccable. During his visit, he was amused when a British reporter said the American yachtsman must have felt especially at home in Plymouth, England, because of his *Mayflower* ancestors. In fact, Lambert's ancestors had reached America before the Pilgrims, arriving in Virginia on the *Francis Bonaventure* in 1619.

Lambert took to England not one but two yachts: the big, beautiful 32-year-old schooner *Atlantic* and the handsome J-boat *Yankee*, a racing vessel that he had brought along to try in the summer's regattas. When *Atlantic* anchored at Gosport, near Portsmouth, Lambert received an impressive greeting on his yacht from an Officer of the Day dressed in full regalia—including a sword that tangled with the officer's legs after he had had a few of Lambert's cocktails. But the yachtsman was more intrigued when he was "commanded" (as royal invitations were expressed) to come to dinner aboard *Victoria and Albert III.*

His irreverent American companions sarcastically saluted Lambert as he departed in evening dress in *Atlantic's* tender. And Lambert committed a *faux pas* right at the start: Approaching the high-sided royal yacht, he nosed up to the starboard gangway, only to be waved off by a deck hand's "discreet arm," as he put it. *Victoria and Albert III* had two gangways, and the starboard was used by no one but the Royal Family.

The port gangway was carpeted. At the first landing, Lambert was formally received by Sir Philip Hunloke, the captain of *Britannia*. Sir Philip ushered the King's guest to the Master of the Household in a reception room where the other guests were already standing about. The

George V (in profile) faces Queen Mary and Princess Mary, both in yachting caps, as a royal yachting party gathers around the binnacle of Britannia off Cowes in the 1920s. The decision of the King a year earlier to refurbish the 221-ton royal cutter stimulated a postwar revival of yachting in England.

Master of the Household presented a diagram of the dinner table for that night, so everyone would know where to sit. A few moments later came an announcement that Their Majesties were approaching.

George V in dinner jacket and Queen Mary in a long gown and magnificent choker moved grandly down the line, shaking hands as their guests bowed and curtsied. With no more ado, the royal couple led everyone into *Victoria and Albert's* dining saloon *(pages 154-155)*. Lambert had the place of honor on the Queen's right. He was relieved to find on his other side the wife of Sir Ralph Gore, a yachting friend. Lady Gore helped put him at ease: Since it would not do to be looking away when the Queen had something to say, Lady Gore promised to alert Lambert when the Queen turned to him. "Fine!" said Lambert. "When you see the Queen turning just say 'Lee-ho' "—the British term for coming about. The system worked, Lambert reported, since the Queen, "slower in stays, would make a more magnificent maneuver" than he would.

With waiters bustling about (there were 350 servants and crew aboard *Victoria and Albert III)*, the dinner proceeded to a stately conclusion. The Queen and the ladies retired to their saloon, and the King and the gentlemen lighted their cigars and passed the port. King George turned to Lambert and asked if he could visit the American's two yachts.

The next morning Lambert was visited by Hunloke, whose functions also included royal security; he asked for the names and background of every guest on *Atlantic* (there were none on *Yankee)*. At 11:30 a.m., *Yankee's* crew was mustered on deck to do their best imitation of a Royal Navy salute as George V climbed aboard. The King went all through the big J-boat, asking about every unfamiliar piece of gear. At one point, a passing vessel erupted with cheers as her passengers recognized His Majesty hanging over the American yacht's bow examining one of the forestays. George V waved back. The royal presence, however, was too much for *Yankee's* steward; when the King asked him a few questions, the steward stammered, "Yes, His Highness!" and " No, His Highness!'" Accompanying the King to *Atlantic,* Lambert was amused to see that his American guests, so taunting the night before, were now drawn up in ranks like sailors, rigidly erect with their hands at their sides.

The visit went well—at least in part because these particular Americans were so scrupulously respectful in behavior. Regrettably, George V could not always count on his own subjects to comport themselves properly at Cowes. The King was horrified one Sunday morning when the wife of a titled British yachtsman appeared in a scarlet bathing suit and dived from the deck of her yacht in full view of the pleasure fleet. Her husband was blackballed by the squadron. But the incident that evidently vexed George V the most was precipitated by, of all people, his wife.

Taking tea one Cowes Week afternoon with Lady Baring, Queen Mary overheard the younger set describing the latest water sport: aquaplaning—riding on a board pulled by a speedboat. One of the aquaplaners was Lady Baring's daughter Poppy. Intrigued, the Queen suggested that the next time they went aquaplaning they come near enough to the royal yacht so that she could see what this new stunt was like.

The next afternoon George V, annoyed by a loud, snarling noise nearby, looked out a porthole and saw Poppy Baring and Lady Glanaris

Mainwaring, both in tight-fitting bathing suits, zooming around and around *Victoria and Albert III* on aquaplanes towed by a huge speedboat. As Lady Mainwaring roared under the royal yacht's stern, she glanced up and caught the eye of the King; his look must have curled the hair under her cap. At her signal, the speedboat raced away. Shortly thereafter, Royal Yacht Squadron Vice Commodore Sir Richard "Tiggy" Williams-Bulkeley received a royal message deploring: (1) young ladies in tight bathing suits, (2) noisy motorboats and (3) encroachments on the privacy of the royal yacht. Evidently the Queen intervened, because Lady Mainwaring and her husband, Sir Harry, were among the guests at dinner aboard *Victoria and Albert III* a few nights later. The King took the opportunity to repeat his disapproval of such antics. Lady Mainwaring realized with surprise that His Majesty did not know that Queen Mary had been on deck waving to them during the entire performance.

Gerard Lambert and his friends notwithstanding, visiting Americans did little to enhance sobriety or support protocol at Cowes. The flapper fad crossed the Atlantic, and squadron members were shocked in the summer of 1924 to see a woman guest walk onto the squadron lawn in a sweater and sailor pants. A rules-committee meeting was called, and a new ordinance was voted: Any lady wearing trousers was forbidden entrance to the squadron grounds. A similar emergency occurred when a member of the squadron discovered a woman in the writing room, sitting at a desk calmly doing her correspondence. The nearest members gathered and conferred in whispers about what to do. Obviously she was an American who did not know that women were not allowed in the building. Unwilling to confront her themselves, the members ordered a steward to expel her politely while they scurried from the scene.

Another American was not so innocent. While the Duke of Leeds was showing a group of visiting yachtsmen and their wives around his steam yacht *Aries*, one of the women lagged behind and filched a cookie from a silver container, dropping it into her purse. Noticing that she had been seen by English yachtsman Anthony Heckstall-Smith—who later recorded the episode—she said, "I guess they'll be tickled to death when I get back home and tell them that it belonged to a real live Dook." Heckstall-Smith suggested that she get Dolly—as the Duke of Leeds was known to his friends—to autograph the cookie, but his sarcasm was lost on the visitor. "I just wouldn't have the nerve," she replied with a sigh.

To many American visitors, the titled British yachtsmen were as puzzling as they were fascinating. Heckstall-Smith, who became the prime raconteur of these giddy years at Cowes, found himself helping an American woman identify some British yachts lying off Cowes.

"Who owns that one over there with the black and white ports and the fancy rig?" she asked.

"Ernest Guinness," Heckstall-Smith answered.

"What, the guy that makes the guinness?"

"The same."

The woman pressed on. "And that cute little black steam yacht?"

"That," Heckstall-Smith responded, "belongs to Richard Hennessy."

"Hennessy's brandy?"

"The same family."

The younger generation added a dash of the flapper era to Cowes during the 1920s. Here Helen "Poppy" Baring (right) and Lady Loughborough ride in the rumble seat and the Honorable Mrs. Lionel Tennyson sits beside Poppy's brother in his rakish roadster.

Bearing down on Victoria and Albert III, two Cowes vacationers wave at the royal yacht. King George V disliked the informality of the '20s and the frequent intrusions on his privacy.

"What about that big white ketch?" the woman asked.

"That's *Cariad*. She belongs to John Gretton." Heckstall-Smith could not resist adding, " He makes the beer called Bass."

Incredulous, she demanded, "But they're all flying the White Ensign, and that means they're all members of the Royal Yacht Squadron?"

"Correct" Heckstall-Smith answered. "You're learning fast."

Cowes yachtsmen jokingly referred to Guinness, Hennessy and Gretton as the "Beerage." But to an American accustomed to Prohibition, anyone who sold liquor was a bootlegger or a gangster, probably both.

"But I just don't understand," she said. "You say all these guys make hootch and yet they're members of this club?"

"Yes, they're all members," Heckstall-Smith replied.

" No kiddin'!" she said. "And they told me this was a high-hat club!"

Vulgar Americans and flappers, aquaplaners and the Beerage—all these signs of changing times at Cowes were bad enough. But the horror of horrors for the veteran yachtsmen was the news in 1925 that Castle

Persian carpets, silk curtains, greenery and glittering silver enhance the state dining cabin of Victoria and Albert III, the finest steam yacht afloat at the turn of the century.

Rock, the house right across the street from the squadron, had been bought by none other than the notorious Rosa Lewis. Rosa was proprietor of London's Cavendish Hotel, known as the proper place for gentlemen to commit their improprieties. (Rosa herself, of working-class birth, was said to have been a mistress of Edward VII at one time, and it was rumored that Edward had given her the hotel.)

From the moment she moved into what she called her "little place" at Cowes, Rosa was an irreverent and disruptive presence. Nearly every night the staid silence of the area was shattered by the noise from Castle Rock, crowded with an assortment of actresses, young British bloods, elderly peers and free-spending Americans who were forever buying rounds of drinks. Like moths to a flame, some of the more adventurous squadron members were drawn across the street to Rosa's roulette parties. These festivities lasted most of the night, and Rosa presided over them with a chaotic kind of discipline. The free-flowing food, liquor and fun attracted even one or two Princes of the Royal Family. They could count on Rosa not to reveal their indiscretion to George V, but they found that royal rank conferred no privilege at Castle Rock. When a young Prince asked for a private room, Rosa wheeled on him. "A private room? A *private* room, did you say? Whatever for? If my friends aren't good enough for you to mix with, my boy, you know what you can do."

Rosa took particular delight in denigrating royalty and aristocracy and in puncturing the pomposity of the squadron members. Sitting in her glass-fronted garden house, sipping champagne and watching the pretentious parade on the squadron lawn, she would point out a dignified yachtsman and murmur to everyone present: "Silly old man! If his wife knew what I know about 'im she'd take an 'airbrush to 'im."

At first the squadron made an uneasy agreement with its new neighbor: Since no women were permitted inside the clubhouse and there were no other toilet facilities handy, Rosa rented to the squadron a ballroom building in her garden. It became a "Ladies' Annexe," and was visited by more and more ladies. As Rosa delicately put it, "While they won't 'ave me on their old lawn, I 'ave to let their lady friends into my garden for their personal convenience, as you might say."

The women's issue at the squadron meanwhile escalated, with a few younger members, urged by their wives, campaigning for new rules admitting women into the clubhouse. At first they were allowed on rare occasions to view the squadron's trophies—escorted by members, of course—and to watch the fireworks from the covered platform on the waterfront on the last evening of the regatta. But the campaign for ladies' privileges became intense—enlivened by an incident that made some of the older members apoplectic. One Cowes Week morning, early-rising yachtsmen looked across the anchorage to see a pair of pink crepe de Chine panties flying at the tip of the Royal Yacht Squadron's masthead. The spectacle did not last long. Soon the squadron's imperturbable signalman, a venerable employee named Wagstaff, marched to the mast, lowered the flag of defiance and, without changing expression, hoisted the squadron's burgee. A search for the miscreant was unsuccessful.

Yachtswomen's rights were finally taken up in 1932 by one of the most conservative members, Lord Albemarle, who proposed that ladies be

Rosa Lewis presents a dignified mien in a 1927 photograph. But the racy parties she often gave at Castle Rock in Cowes embarrassed the stuffier members of the Royal Yacht Squadron across the street.

allowed to have luncheon and dinner "in the small room at the west end of the Castle," but only in the off-season, when they were unlikely to have a disruptive effect (a grand total of 17 members had entered the clubhouse the previous winter). With so prestigious a member as Albemarle on the ladies' side, Williams-Bulkeley, who now was commodore, threw in his support, and by a vote of 41 to 25, ladies were at last permitted inside the premises of the Royal Yacht Squadron—through a separate entrance to the Castle. No women—except Queens Victoria and Elizabeth II—were admitted to membership until 1964, when female relatives of members were finally granted associate membership.

The Ladies' Annexe in Rosa Lewis' garden ballroom was also still available; the squadron by now had bought it. But Rosa kept her house and garden, and continued to embarrass the members. The serenity of one Cowes Week Sunday was destroyed when Rosa was rowed out to visit an American yacht. Clad in a flowing pink gown and a picture hat, she rose from the rowboat in a bosun's chair, and her American hosts, Dan Simonds and John Parkinson, were so struck by the sight that they hauled her to the mast top and kept her there. While Rosa screeched obscenities, British yachtsmen gasped and watched through their telescopes. It was Rosa who, when she returned to the Cavendish in the late 1930s, delivered the obituary on the golden age at Cowes. "The fun's all over m'dear. We won't none of us see no more of that sort of thing."

In America, the years after World War I seemed to promise an endless increase of yachting fun. It was, of course, fun with a purpose, as the American sociologist Thorstein Veblen had pointed out in his *Theory of the Leisure Class*, published in 1899. Veblen wrote that "to gain and hold the esteem of men it is not sufficient merely to possess wealth or power. The wealth or power must be put in evidence." His memorable phrase for this manifestation was "conspicuous consumption," which, he explained, "is a means of reputability to the gentleman of leisure."

America enjoyed a giddy postwar boom, and yachtsmen proved Veblen's theory as never before, building the biggest, fastest, most ostentatious pleasure craft the world would ever see. Not the least of the factors contributing to this phenomenon was the perfection of the diesel-powered engine, which produced far more energy than steam did.

Steam did not disappear immediately. In 1904, for example, William K. Vanderbilt Jr. had a steam yacht resembling the torpedo boats used during the War. When this proved too slow for him, he took her to naval architect Clinton Crane, who installed bigger steam boilers. That did the trick; and the yacht's name, *Tarantula*, was regarded as an apt one by every yachtsman near her; she left such a high, rolling wake that Vanderbilt was sued for damages by boat owners all up and down the East River.

But by 1922, Willie, as he was known, traded up to a diesel yacht. She had been built as a sloop of war in England in 1917. Vanderbilt named her *Ara* and installed two 1,200-horsepower diesel engines capable of driving her at a cruising speed of 14½ knots for 5,000 miles. *Ara* was a seaworthy vessel with a steel-plated hull; and Vanderbilt, who had a master's certificate and knew his navigation, saw that she was outfitted with the best equipment, including one of the first examples of an automatic pilot, a device Willie called "Metal Mike." He wrote that Metal Mike steered *Ara* "automatically and truer to course than any quartermaster could." The yacht also had a fire-alarm system and a wireless apparatus with a 2,500-mile range, allowing Vanderbilt to maintain contact with land at all times. Information received by the wireless was used to publish a daily shipboard paper titled *The Ara Daily News*.

Besides reading their own paper, Willie's guests could while away their time at the Steinway grand piano in the Adam-period music room or browse in the yacht's library. They could promenade on the 212-foot deck or retire to one of the six staterooms, each with a private bath. Cardplayers had a special room for their games, well ventilated to get rid of pipe and cigar smoke. *Ara's* dispensary was as complete as that of a drugstore, and her staff included a doctor. She also was equipped for oceanographic explorations, complete with aquariums *(pages 160-161)*.

In 1927, Vanderbilt took *Ara* on an eight-month Mediterranean cruise. He and his guests swam over the side, watched movies of Willie's other cruises, dined on the awninged deck, enjoyed the scenery and made short trips ashore. One morning Vanderbilt woke his guests at 3 a.m. to watch a volcanic eruption on Stromboli Island off Italy—only to have the volcano cease as the sleepy-eyed guests came grumbling on deck. On a summer night when *Ara* was anchored in the open roadstead off Athens' port of Piraeus to escape the inner harbor's mosquitoes, a firing exercise by the Greek Navy grazed the yacht.

In their pursuit of pleasure, American millionaires furnished their yachts with every amenity. In addition to the customary grand saloons warmed by marble-manteled fireplaces, there were gymnasiums, swimming pools and movie theaters. *Lounger IV*, built for inventor James Hammond, featured a bed that rose when a lever was pushed, allowing the owner to look out the porthole without sitting up.

A classic example of luxury afloat was *Lyndonia*, built in 1920 for Cyrus H. K. Curtis, publisher of *The Saturday Evening Post*. Slim and graceful, *Lyndonia* measured 230 feet from her scroll-decorated clipper bow to her wide, covered fantail. Each cabin and stateroom was furnished with antiques of a different period. The Curtises' stateroom was done in Adam period. The main saloon was William and Mary, with heavy walnut paneling, electric candelabra and plate-glass windows instead of portholes. The smoking room was Tudor, with a great oak desk and scattered leather armchairs. *Lyndonia* also had seven tiled bathrooms, and her silk-curtained, Jacobean dining saloon "might have been transplanted from the St. Regis," wrote a *Yachting* reporter. He nominated the vessel as "yacht of the year."

A particular feature of many 1920s yachts was the bar. The United States millionaires, even more than most Americans at the time, openly flouted Prohibition, and a wealthy man's choice of bootlegger was as important as his choice of tailor. Indeed, one of the attractions of a yacht during Prohibition was the fact that liquor could be drunk legally outside the three-mile limit off the coast of the United States. A few yacht owners, feeling a need for discretion closer to shore, fitted their vessels with hidden bars. Some of these became legendary. One yacht, for example, had a control panel with buttons that not only served to call servants or turn on music, lights, heat or fans, but also would whisk aside a panel to reveal a bar and would even lower a wall between the owner's stateroom and that of the woman occupying the stateroom next to his.

It was a time when American tycoons could indulge any whim, however expensive. Newspaper publisher Joseph Pulitzer, who was nearly blind, insisted that his 304-foot steam yacht *Liberty* have rounded corners in all the passageways and no steps on deck. Sensitive to noise, he had the yacht's engine room and bulkheads heavily soundproofed; and when Pulitzer was aboard—he liked to cruise aimlessly off the United States coast, keeping in touch with his office by radio—the deck hands were forbidden to do any noisy work except during specified hours.

One of the fussiest yacht owners on record was tin magnate William B. Leeds. After he and naval architect Clinton Crane had agreed on the plans for his new steamer *Noma*, Leeds immediately started having second thoughts and continued to do so throughout her construction. He altered the yacht's length, then asked for more speed than the planned 17 knots. He ordered custom-designed porcelain bathtubs after deciding that the ones called for were too small. Crane tried to point out that each change added to the cost, but Leeds kept making alterations, finally calling in an architect who knew nothing about ships to design the woodwork of the grand saloon and the other large cabins. With no concern for weight, the architect produced, and Leeds insisted on, a massive structure of joinery decorated with carved dolphins, starfish and scallop shells. Crane feared that, with all these weighty additions, the 252-foot yacht would not make the speed he had promised. But she did, and Leeds happily paid more than half a million dollars for his *Noma*.

Leeds had a business partner, Daniel G. Reid, who asked Crane to build a sister ship to *Noma*. While he gave Crane less trouble than Leeds had, Reid could be a terror to his crew because of his temper. "Daniel Reid, when sober, was one of the mildest mannered men you ever saw," Crane recalled. But one evening aboard his new yacht *Rheclair*, Reid got a head start on the cocktails while waiting for his dinner guests to come out to the anchorage. Inspecting the dinner table and discerning a flaw in the arrangement, Reid flew into a rage, yanked the damask tablecloth and sent the silver, china and glassware flying, then hustled the steward up the companionway and threw him over the side into Oyster Bay harbor, just as guests arrived in the launch. The guests rescued the steward; but, Crane reported, "dinner was considerably delayed."

Yachting in the 1920s tended to attract, as well as breed, eccentrics, and not only in the United States. One man who had occasion to deal with many of them was Herbert E. Julyan, a London-based broker of luxury yachts. Among his clients, Julyan recalled in his memoirs, was a landlubber who kept getting lost belowdecks; finally, the owner had the interior woodwork on one side painted white and on the other side blue so he could find his way about. Another client was a seasickness-prone financier who purchased a yacht anyway because, as he explained, "I bought a big telescope and as soon as I opened it I thought I would like a yacht," presumably the better to see the horizon.

Impulse buying took many forms, including the delayed version that occurred in 1930 when Julyan endeavored to sell the 248-foot yacht

Cruises in the cause of science

One yachtsman who was not content simply to lounge on his vessel's fantail was William K. Vanderbilt Jr. Aboard his 212-foot *Ara* he combined pleasure with scientific investigation during cruises throughout the world. In the process, he became an amateur ichthyologist of note, discovering many new species of marine life, which he brought home to his private museum at Northport, on Long Island.

A voyage to the Galápagos Islands in 1926 was particularly memorable. Vanderbilt took along four guests, a 33-man crew, a professional fisherman, a photographer (who was provided with a darkroom), and even an artist to record the colors of fishes before they faded.

In addition to ichthyological species, the yachting party studied such local creatures as penguins and tortoises. Meanwhile, curious pelicans flocked to study the yachtsmen, and at one island baby iguanas climbed onto their mothers' backs for a better look at the party.

The 1926 expedition bagged some 25 hitherto unknown marine specimens. But Vanderbilt's happiest catch was one of the passengers: A year later he and Rosalind Warburton divorced their spouses and were married.

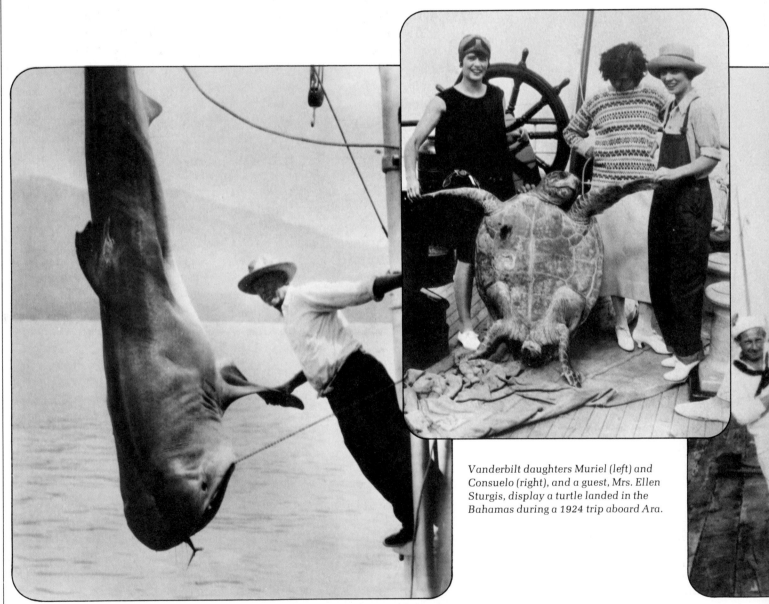

Vanderbilt daughters Muriel (left) and Consuelo (right), and a guest, Mrs. Ellen Sturgis, display a turtle landed in the Bahamas during a 1924 trip aboard Ara.

Professional fisherman Charlie Thompson grasps the fin of a 16-foot tiger shark that was caught off James Island in the Galápagos during Ara's 1926 cruise.

Her booms extended to hold her launches and nets, *Ara* lies at anchor in the Galápagos Islands. Vanderbilt used the nets for fishing and for passengers' protection from sharks while swimming.

Vanderbilt (center) poses as stiffly as any neophyte fisherman against the backdrop of a 16-foot-wide manta ray that was a prize of his 1924 outing.

Reveler. The yacht broker aroused the interest of a number of American businessmen, including Charles McCann, head of the Woolworth retail chain. *Reveler* sat at a dock in Southampton, England, and McCann was in London on business, but claimed not to have time to inspect her. He asked Julyan to have the yacht brought alongside the passenger ship *Bremen* so he could look at her as he sailed past on his way to New York. Julyan replied that this would cost £400. McCann changed his mind and, for the first time, asked the price of the yacht. Julyan quoted a figure of £75,000. McCann exploded, " Nobody can afford to keep a yacht like that nowadays!" Julyan waited until the *Bremen* sailed, then cabled his representative in New York to meet McCann on his arrival. As he had guessed, McCann had cooled down. He bought *Reveler*, renamed her *Chalena*, furnished her luxuriously and enjoyed her for a decade.

Not all the beneficiaries of America's boom felt wealthy enough to buy yachts; indeed, one young Rockefeller, asked why he did not have a yacht, replied, "Who do you think we are? Vanderbilts?" But some millionaires made even the Vanderbilts look parsimonious when it came to luxury craft. Emily Roebling Cadwalader, whose fortune came from the wire-and-cable company that built the Brooklyn Bridge, was a case in point. She commissioned three yachts, all named *Savarona*. The first one seemed cramped at 185 feet, so Mrs. Cadwalader invested two million dollars in trading up to *Savarona II*, which was launched in 1928. The new *Savarona* was 294 feet long, required a crew of 41 and cost about $200,000 a year to maintain. Among her modern improvements were gyrostabilizers—fins that could be extended from the hull to keep her steady in a heavy sea. Mrs. Cadwalader found they also could be manipulated to make the yacht roll at anchor, and she enjoyed demonstrating seagoing conditions to her guests while sitting in the harbor having cocktails. *Savarona II* also had black marble bathrooms with gold fixtures; the fixtures were a true economy, a friend, Mrs. Edward T. Stotesbury, explained, because they did not require daily polishing.

Still, 294 feet of floating splendor failed to satisfy Mrs. Cadwalader. So she commissioned the largest nonroyal yacht ever built. *Savarona III* was 408 feet long and rated at 4,646 tons—as large as an ocean liner. She cost four million dollars, carried a crew of 83 and could average 17 knots. Eleven watertight bulkheads ensured the yacht's safety. In her enormous hull were 12 spacious staterooms, each with a private bath or shower, of course. Mrs. Cadwalader's own suite was so large that it was called an apartment. But size had its drawbacks: Because of the yacht's 20-foot draft, she could enter only major commercial ports. At the resorts Mrs. Cadwalader liked to visit, *Savarona III* anchored in the roadstead and the yachting party made their way ashore in tenders.

In creating this behemoth, the wire-and-cable heiress was the victim of bad timing. *Savarona III* was launched in 1931, when the nation was sinking into the depths of the Depression. Moreover, America's great fortunes were being squeezed by increases in income-tax rates. In Mrs. Cadwalader's case, the combination of lowered income and higher taxes meant that she had to keep her huge yacht outside the continental limits of the United States to avoid the enormous import duties that even she could ill afford. *Savarona III* had been built in Germany; she never came

Power in the hold: "Alva's" mighty diesels

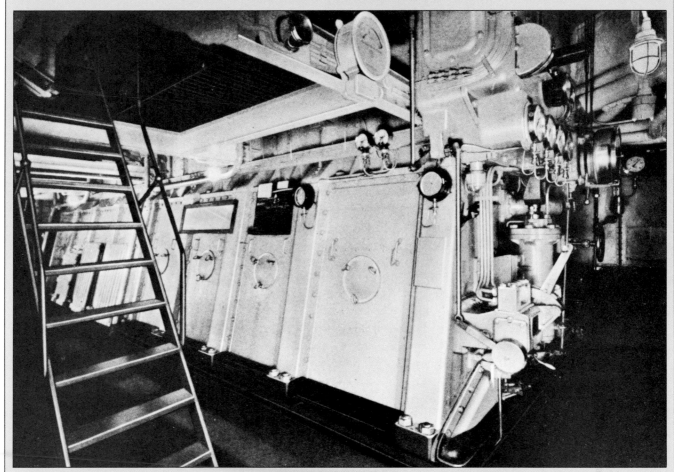

Alva's main engines weighed 300 tons. To support them, the yacht had heavy transverse bulkheads and extra-thick hull plating.

The evolution of the power-driven yacht reached an awesome new level in the gleaming bank of diesel engines shown above, housed in William K. Vanderbilt Jr.'s *Alva*. A 264-foot steel-hulled vessel, *Alva* was powered by two 2,100-horsepower monsters that drove her 3,600 tons at speeds up to 17 knots.

By 1930, when *Alva* was being constructed, the marine diesel engine—operating on a principle similar to that of the gasoline engine but able to use less-combustible (therefore safer) fuel—was almost a quarter of a century old: It had first been used at sea in the Dutch tanker *Vulcanus* in 1910. Yachtsmen did not immediately take to diesels: The newfangled power plants produced more noise and vibration than a steam engine did. But these problems were soon alleviated, and even die-hard traditionalists were forced to admit the clear superiority of diesels over steam in some respects. Diesel engines delivered more power from their fuel than coal-burning steam engines did, thus saving

space and improving performance; they were also cleaner.

Diesel power was particularly appealing to American yachtsmen, who—in contrast with their European counterparts—were more interested in speed than in quiet operation. Vanderbilt had already learned the advantages of this type of engine in his twin-diesel *Ara (pages 157-158)*, and when he commissioned the Krupp-Germaniawerft yard in Kiel to build his new *Alva*, he not only specified twin diesels as the main power plant but ordered duplicate diesels installed in case the main units failed. The result, he noted, was "the most powerfully constructed yacht in existence."

Alva burned 12 tons of fuel a day, but her tanks could carry enough for 15,000 miles of travel without stopping to refuel. In 1931 her owner put the engines' stamina to a stern test when he circumnavigated the world in less than a year. Not one mechanical mishap marred the trip—a 38,000-mile endurance run that Vanderbilt boasted was unprecedented in yachting annals.

to the United States. Mrs. Cadwalader did take a few cruises aboard her palatial plaything, in the Atlantic, around Europe and once around South America. But by the mid-1930s, *Savarona III* was the greatest white elephant of luxury yachting—for sale at a third of her building cost and with no takers. She was finally bought by the Turkish government in 1938, for a quarter of what Mrs. Cadwalader had paid for her.

The timing was no better for the owners of another spectacular yacht, but the Depression had less effect on them. Wall Street broker E. F. Hutton had in the early 1920s taken a leave from his firm and become chairman of the board of the Postum Cereal Company, after marrying the founder's daughter, millionairess Marjorie Merriweather Post. During those years, the Huttons entertained grandly aboard their 203-foot schooner *Hussar*, whose main saloon featured a grand piano and an electric fireplace with a mantel of Siena marble. Like Mrs. Cadwalader, the Huttons longed for an even larger vessel; and in 1931 they launched another *Hussar*, one of the most beautiful yachts ever built. She measured 316 feet from her clipper bow to her graceful counter. Her diesel engines, able to move her at 14 knots, were supplemented by four towering masts. She was bark-rigged, with square sails on her three forward masts and a fore-and-aft mizzen. Her total sail area was 35,822 square feet, comparable to that of the clipper ships of the previous century.

The largest nonroyal yacht ever built, 408-foot Savarona III was commissioned just before the stock-market crash in 1929 by Emily Roebling Cadwalader, granddaughter of the builder of the Brooklyn Bridge. Mrs. Cadwalader used her for two years; she wound up as a Turkish Navy training ship.

The second *Hussar* was as luxurious belowdecks as any yacht had ever been, with marble bathrooms, parquet floors and antique furniture. Because of her huge sail area as well as her lavish accommodations, she required a crew of 72, who were outfitted with new uniforms twice a year. And when the deepening Depression made the yacht's upkeep seem extravagant, Mrs. Hutton explained that it was the duty of those who could afford it to spend money to help revive the economy. *Hussar's* owners were divorced in 1935. Marjorie Post Hutton kept the yacht, renaming it *Sea Cloud* when she married Joseph Davies the same year.

Yachting actually helped one millionaire survive the Crash of 1929 and the hard years afterward. Woolens manufacturer Julius Forstmann set out on his yacht *Orion* in early 1929, taking his son Julius on a round-the-world cruise as part of his education. At port after port the senior Forstmann saw bulging waterfront warehouses—signs of an international market glut due to declining purchasing power. By the time *Orion* had worked her way through Asia and across the Pacific to Honolulu, it was early October, 1929. Forstmann called his broker in New York and directed him to sell the entire Forstmann portfolio. Ten days later he called again, to be sure his orders had been followed. His broker replied that he had not sold anything. "Aren't you glad?" he asked. "Everything's gone up ten points." Blistering the wires, Forstmann fired the broker and got another, who liquidated the portfolio. Two weeks later, on October 24, the bottom fell out of the New York stock market.

A few other multimillionaires withstood the immediate effects of the first stock-market plunge, notably J. P. Morgan Jr., who temporarily tried to support the market and stem the panic. But by 1931 Morgan paid no income taxes because he did not have enough income. His fourth *Corsair*, built the previous year at a cost of $2.5 million, was laid up for a year in 1935. This *Corsair*—344 feet long and nearly as large as *Savarona III*—was described by yachting author Erik Hofman as "the crown at the end of the steam yacht era."

Corsair, Hussar, Savarona—such yachts were the last magnificent gesture of conspicuous consumption. Not only were they suddenly too expensive, they also now constituted an affront to an impoverished world. Indeed, a similar example of extravagance backfired when Vincent Astor entertained President Franklin D. Roosevelt aboard his 264-foot *Nourmahal*. The President, commenting on the yacht's sumptuousness, remarked rather unkindly that if America's wealthy men could afford such luxuries, perhaps they were not yet taxed enough.

Conspicuous consumption in the old style was thus not only beyond most yachtsmen's means but a bad policy as well. It took a worldwide Depression to bring about the change, but the change was permanent. In 1930 there had been 81 yachts of 200 tons or more in the New York Yacht Club fleet; a decade later, there were half that many. And World War II completed what the Depression had begun. When in 1949 J. P. Morgan Jr.'s son Henry became the fourth Morgan to be elected commodore of the New York Yacht Club, his flagship was not a 300-foot luxury yacht but a mere 62-foot cutter named *Djinn*. She was no bigger—and certainly a lot less pretentious—than the royal barge that had borne Cleopatra to her rendezvous with Mark Antony almost two thousand years earlier.

"Sea Cloud" versus "Nabila"—a contrast in grandeur

With all sails set, Sea Cloud could clip off 165 miles in a day. The yacht also had a 6,000 hp diesel-electric power plant.

If one luxury yacht can be said to embody the glories of yesteryear, the lovely 316-foot square-rigger *Sea Cloud,* commissioned by Mrs. Marjorie Post Hutton in 1931, might well deserve the honor. By a fluke, *Sea Cloud* was still sailing the seas in the 1980s. In 1978 a German captain, Hartmut Packsburg, found her rusting in Panama harbor, a near-derelict. He and a consortium of German businessmen restored her for seven million dollars and chartered her for cruising.

Much of her sailing was done in the Mediterranean, where she might cross paths with the most opulent modern yacht afloat, Saudi Arabian businessman Adnan Khashoggi's 280-foot *Nabila (right).* The differences in seaborne splendor over half a century—from *Sea Cloud's* original opulence of walnut paneling and antique furnishings to *Nabila's* sleek lushness of mirror surfaces and suede sofas—are compared in the photographs on the following pages.

Nabila was built with two 3,000 hp diesels. The winglike protrusion from the upper deck is one of two matching air vents for the engines and generators.

Mrs. Hutton's stateroom on Sea Cloud boasted a bed with canopied headboard, antiques, a fireplace and a chandeliered ceiling.

Adnan Khashoggi's stateroom on Nabila had a mirrored ceiling, abstract art and bedside controls for television and the curtains.

Sea Cloud's main saloon resembled a country-house library, with a marble-manteled fireplace and a grand piano by the entrance to the dining room.

In this view the spacious main saloon of Nabila is lighted from above, furnished with suede-covered couches and draped with Thai wall hangings.

Game fish adorned the paneling of Sea Cloud's dining saloon. The room also featured an Oriental rug and Georgian chairs.

Mrs. Hutton's bathroom had a marble basin and tub. The bath mat carried the yacht's first name, Hussar, changed to Sea Cloud in 1935.

Nabila's dining room gleams with a long, Chinese-laquered table and 18 chairs of white leather. The yacht's design incorporated eight suites for guests.

A lady's bathroom aboard Nabila is fitted with a copper basin and toilet compartment of lapis lazuli (center). The marble tub has a miniature waterfall.

Acknowledgments

The index for this book was prepared by Gale Linck Partoyan. The editors would like to thank artist Peter McGinn (endpaper maps).

The editors also wish to thank: In France: Le Havre—J. F. Mezisen; Paris—Claude Bréguet, Raymond Didier, Association du Souvenir de Ferdinand de Lesseps et de Canal de Suez; Philippe Capron, Compagnie Financière de Suez; Marjolaine Matikhine, Director for Historical Studies, Claude Bellarbre, Jacques Chantriot, Catherine Touny, Musée de la Marine. In Italy: Genoa—Beppe Croce, President, Yacht Club Italiano; Rome—Luigi Sturchio; Viareggio—Cantieri Navali Fratelli Benetti, Cantiere Navale M. B. Benetti. In Spain: Málaga—Carlos Gomez Raggio, President, Manuel Rubio Montoro, Real Club Mediterraneo. In Sweden: Göteborgs—Maria Seldén-Bengtsson, Göteborgs Kungliga Segel Sällskap. In the United Kingdom: Bedfordshire—Lavinia Wellicome, Curator, Woburn Abbey; Berkshire—Frances Dimond, Assistant Registrar, Royal Archive, Melissa Bonn, Print Room, Royal Library, Windsor Castle; Cowes, Isle of Wight—Spencer Herapath, Honorary Custodian of Pictures, Major R. P. Rising, Secretary, Royal Yacht Squadron; London—Marjorie Willis, BBC Hulton Picture Library; R. Williams, Department of Prints and Drawings, British Museum; E.H.H. Archibald, Curator of Oil Paintings, David Lyon, Curator, Draught Room, Joan Moore, Executive Officer, Photographic Sales, Stephen Riley, Curator of Models, Department of Ships, Roger Quarm, Department of Pictures, National Maritime Museum; Captain A. R. Ward, Secretary, Royal Thames Yacht Club; J. Roome, Department of Ships, Science Museum. In West Germany: Kiel—Admiral Hans-Rudolf Rösing.

The editors also wish to thank: In the United States: Cambridge, Massachusetts—Professor Emeritus William Avery Baker, Hart Nautical Museum, Massachusetts Institute of Technology; Centerport, New York—Alexander J. Brandshaft, Executive Director, Diane Englot, Assistant Curator, Vanderbilt Museum; Easthampton, New York—Dina Merrill; Mystic, Connecticut—Philip Budlong, Registrar, Amy German, Photographic Cataloguer, Georgia Hamilton, Senior Cataloguer, Mystic Seaport Museum; Newport, Rhode Island—John Mecray, Monique M. Panaggio, Preservation Society of Newport County; Newport News, Virginia—Charlotte Valentine, Library Assistant, Lois Oglesby, Curatorial Assistant, Mariners Museum; New York, New York—Mrs. E. Soschin, Permissions, Charles Scribner's Sons, Joseph Conlin, Stanley Rosenfeld, Heather Hanley, Morris Rosenfeld & Sons, Kathy Butska, Print Department, Museum of the City of New York, New York Public Library Office of Special Collections, Sohei Hohri, Librarian, New York Yacht Club; Princeton, New Jersey—Edward Fischer, Ridge Press; Salem, Massachusetts—Paul Winfisky, Print Collection, Kathy Flynn, Photographic Assistant, Barbara Edkins, Librarian, Mark Sexton, Museum Photographer, Peabody Museum of Salem.

Particularly valuable sources of quotations were *The History of Yachting, 1600-1815* by Arthur H. Clark, New York Yacht Club and G. P. Putnam's Sons, New York, 1904; *The Story of George Crowninshield's Yacht Cleopatra's Barge* edited by Francis B. Crowninshield, privately printed, Boston, 1913; *Salt-Water Palaces* by Maldwin Drummond, The Viking Press, New York, 1980; *Yachting: A History* by Peter Heaton, B. T. Batsford, London, 1955; and *Sacred Cowes* by Anthony Heckstall-Smith, Allan Wingate, London, 1955.

Bibliography

Atkins, J. B., *Further Memorials of the Royal Yacht Squadron*. London: Geoffrey Bles, 1939.

Ayling, Stanley, *George the Third*. Knopf, 1972.

Bagot, A. G., *Shooting and Yachting in the Mediterranean*. London: W. H. Allen, 1888.

Baker, W. A., *The Engine Powered Vessel*. Grosset & Dunlap, 1965.

Bedford, John, Duke of, *The Flying Duchess*. London: Macdonald, n.d.

Bedford, Mary, Duchess of, *Diaries*. John Gore, ed. Printed for private circulation, London: John Murray, 1938.

Benjamin, Samuel Greene Wheeler, *Sea-Spray; or, Facts and Fancies of a Yachtsman*. Benjamin & Bell, 1887.

Bond, Donald F., ed., *The Spectator*, Vol. 1. Oxford: Clarendon Press, 1965.

Brassey, Mrs. Anna, *Around the World in the Yacht 'Sunbeam'; Our Home on the Ocean for Eleven Months*. Henry Holt, 1880.

Brooks, Jerome E., *The $30,000,000 Cup*. Simon & Schuster, 1958.

Casson, Lionel:
Illustrated History of Ships and Boats. Doubleday, 1964.
Ships and Seamanship in the Ancient World. Princeton University Press, 1971.

Choules, John Overton, *The Cruise of the Steam Yacht North Star*. Gould and Lincoln, 1854.

Clark, Arthur H., *The History of Yachting, 1600-1815*. G. P. Putnam's Sons, 1904.

Condy, Mrs. N. M., *Reminiscences of a Yachting Cruise*. London: Ackerman, 1852.

Cooper, William, *The Yacht Sailor*. London: Hunt, 1876.

Crabtree, Reginald:
The Luxury Yacht from Steam to Diesel. Newton Abbot: David & Charles, 1973.
Royal Yachts of Europe. Newton Abbot: David & Charles, 1975.

Crane, Clinton, *Clinton Crane's Yachting Memories*. D. Van Nostrand, 1952.

Crowninshield, Francis B., ed., *The Story of George Crowninshield's Yacht Cleopatra's Barge*. Privately printed, 1913.

Dear, Ian, *Enterprise to Endeavour*. Dodd, Mead, 1977.

Drummond, Maldwin, *Salt-Water Palaces*. Viking Press, 1980.

Duff, David, *Eugénie and Napoleon III*. William Morrow, 1978.

Falconer, William, *An Universal Dictionary of the Marine*. London: T. Cadell, 1789.

Ferguson, David L., *Cleopatra's Barge: The Crowninshield Story*. Little, Brown, 1976.

Fraser, Antonia, *Royal Charles: Charles II and the Restoration*. Knopf, 1979.

Gavin, C. M., *Royal Yachts*. London: Rich & Cowan, 1932.

Goulaeff, E. E., "The Russian Imperial Yacht *Livadia*." *Journal of the Franklin Institute*, August 1880.

Guest, Montague and William B. Boulton, *The Royal Yacht Squadron*. London: John Murray, 1903.

Heaton, Peter, *Yachting: A History*. London: B. T. Batsford, 1955.

Heckstall-Smith, Anthony, *Sacred Cowes*. London: Allan Wingate, 1955.

Heckstall-Smith, B., "*All Hands on the Mainsheet!*" London: Grant Richards, 1921.

Herapath, Spencer, *The Royal Yacht Squadron 1815-1975*. Cowes: Royal Yacht Squadron, 1976.

Herreshoff, L. Francis, *The Common Sense of Yacht Design*. Caravan-Maritime Books, 1973.

Hofman, Erik, *The Steam Yachts*. John De Graff, 1970.

Hoyt, Edwin P., *The Vanderbilts and Their Fortunes*. Doubleday, 1962.

Irving, John, *The King's Britannia*. London: Seeley Service, 1937.

Julyan, Herbert E., *Sixty Years of Yachts*.

London: Hutchinson, 1950.

Kirkpatrick, Konstance, *The History of the Indian Harbor Yacht Club, 1889-1977.* Indian Harbor Yacht Club, 1978.

Kirtz, Harold, *The Empress Eugénie.* Houghton Mifflin, 1964.

Lamb, Julia, " 'The Commodore' Enjoyed Life—But N.Y. Society Winced." *Smithsonian,* Vol. 9, No. 8, November 1978.

Lambert, Gerard B., *Yankee in England.* Charles Scribner's Sons, 1937.

Longford, Elizabeth, *Queen Victoria: Born to Succeed.* Harper & Row, 1964.

Ludwig, Emil, *Wilhelm Hohenzollern.* G. P. Putnam's Sons, 1927.

Massie, Robert K.:
Nicholas and Alexandra. Dell, 1978.
Peter the Great: His Life and World. Alfred A. Knopf, 1980.

McCutchan, Philip, *Great Yachts.* London: Weidenfeld and Nicolson, 1979.

McGowan, A. P., *Royal Yachts.* London: Her Majesty's Stationery Office, 1977.

O'Connor, Richard, "The Wayward Commodore." *American Heritage,* Vol. 25, June 1974.

Parkinson, John Jr., *The History of the New York Yacht Club.* 2 vols. New York Yacht Club, 1975.

Phillips-Birt, Douglas:
The Cumberland Fleet: Two Hundred Years of Yachting 1775-1975. London: Royal Thames Yacht Club, 1978.
The History of Yachting. Stein and Day, 1974.

Plutarch, *Plutarch's Lives.* Transl. by Bernadotte Perrin, Harvard University Press, 1948.

Priestley, J. B., *The Prince of Pleasure and His Regency.* London: Heinemann, 1969.

Pudney, John, *Suez: De Lessep's Canal.* London: J. M. Dent & Sons, 1968.

Richardson, Joanna, *George the Magnificent: A Portrait of King George IV.* Harcourt, Brace & World, 1966.

Robinson, Bill, *Legendary Yachts.* McKay, 1978.

Rosenfeld, Morris, William H. Taylor and Stanley Rosenfeld, *The Story of American Yachting.* Appleton-Century-Crofts, 1958.

Sackville-West, V., *The Edwardians.* Viking Press, 1961.

Seitz, Don C., *The James Gordon Bennetts: Father and Son.* Bobbs-Merrill, 1928.

The Southampton Town and Country Herald, Isle of Wight Gazette and General Advertiser. August 21, 1826: "The Ball on Board the *Falcon.*"

The Spirit of The Times, September 15, 1900: "A. J. Drexel."

Vanderbilt, William K.:
Fifteen Thousand Miles Cruise with Ara. Privately printed, 1928.
Taking One's Own Ship Around the World. Privately printed, 1929.
To Galápagos on the Ara. Privately printed, 1927.
West Made East with the Loss of a Day. Privately printed, 1933.

Veblen, Thorstein, *The Theory of the Leisure Class.* Viking Press, 1935.

Wallace, William N., *The Macmillan Book of Boating.* Macmillan, 1964.

Watson, Alfred E. T., *King Edward VII as a Sportsman.* London: Longmans, 1911.

Waugh, Alec, *The Lipton Story: A Centennial Biography.* Doubleday, 1950.

Whitehall, Walter Muir, *George Crowninshield's Yacht Cleopatra's Barge.* Peabody Museum, 1959.

Picture Credits

Index

The Luxury Yachts

CANADA

NEWFOUNDLAND

UNITED STATES

NOVA SCOTIA

Hudson River

Salem

Boston

Oyster Bay

New York

Long Island

Newport

NORTH STAR

CLEOPATRA'S BARGE

A T L A N T I C

CORSAIR

80° W.

60° N.

70° W.

60° W.

50° W.

50° N.

40° N.

70° W.

60° W.

50° W.